D1128575

Constancy & Change
in Quaker Philanthropy

A History of the Barrow Cadbury Trust

Merlin Waterson
& Samantha Wyndham

The Barrow Cadbury Trust 2013

No 1

The originals of Nos 1. 2. + 3 were painted in the autumn of 1868 R.C.

No 2

No 3

Birmingham Gazette [illegible] 1869

CADBURY'S CHOCOLATE CRÈMES.—Among the pictorial novelties introduced to the trade this season, few, if any, excel the illustration on Messrs. Cadbury's four-ounce box of chocolate crèmes. It is chaste, yet simple, and consists of a blue-eyed maiden, some six summers old, neatly dressed in a muslin frock trimmed with lace, nursing a cat. It is designed and drawn by Mr. Richard Cadbury (a member of the firm), and reflects great credit upon him for its artistic excellence. The picture is got up in colours by Messrs. Goodall and Co., of London.—*The Grocer.*

Messrs. Cadbury Brothers, of Birmingham, have just introduced two new fancy boxes for their three-ounce size of chocolate crèmes. On one is a pretty marine view—a juvenile on the beach about to test the sailing properties of a fully-rigged toy ship; on the other, an exquisite picture of a mother and child. Both subjects have been designed by Mr. Richard Cadbury, and skilfully worked out by Messrs. Kronheim and Co.—*The Grocer.*

Birmingham Gazette 9 Nov. 69

Robertson's comedy, "Home," has been played to crowded houses in Birmingham during the present week. On the 22nd inst., in the opening scene, Colonel John White (Mr. Sothern) presented Bertie Thompson (Lucy Dorrison's lover) with a conciliatory gift in the shape of a box of Cadbury's Chocolate Crèmes. The dialogue that ensued was as much appreciated by the audience as the box was by the recipient.

The box with the picture of Mother + child was the one presented by Mr Sothern + adopted by him through the whole of the kingdom. R.C.

The original was painted in the Spring of 1869 RC

No 4

No 5

The originals of No 4 + 5 were painted in the Spring of 1870.

Contents

Opposite *Chocolate-box designs by Richard Cadbury,* c.*1868–70: the picture of a small boy holding a yacht is believed to be a portrait of his son, Barrow.*

Foreword *by Professor Sir David Cannadine*

For the best part of two hundred years, Cadbury has been a household name in Birmingham, and it certainly was in my home, as I grew up in the city during the 1950s and 1960s. The husband of a cousin of mine spent his entire working life as a senior manager at Cadburys; my sister for a time worked at Edgbaston High School for Girls, where the governors were chaired by Mrs Laurence Cadbury; and in what would now be termed my 'gap' year between school and university, I worked for twelve weeks on the night shift at Cadburys, packing Easter eggs, and so I was on the firm's payroll when it merged with Schweppes.

But Cadburys has always meant more than cocoa and chocolate, for the family were high-minded Quakers (strongly supporting temperance) and exemplary employers (hence their model factory and workers' housing at Bournville). Across the generations, the Cadburys supported many good and liberal causes: George Cadbury acquired a controlling interest in the *Daily News*, the better to oppose the Boer War; his wife, Dame Elizabeth Cadbury, was devoted to education, youth work and women's welfare; and it was George's nephew Barrow Cadbury who in 1920, and with his wife Geraldine, founded the Trust which still bears his name, drawing its income from shares in the family company.

Opposite
Barrow and Geraldine Cadbury in 1916.

Along with other Quaker families who were also active in the food and confectionary industries, such as the Rowntrees in York and the Frys in Bristol, the Cadburys constituted what was sometimes known as 'the chocolate conscience'. Many of their philanthropic endeavours were individual – and, on occasions, they could be idiosyncratic. But across almost a century, and as this vivid and important book repeatedly makes plain, the Barrow Cadbury Trust has been both an exemplary and a pioneering charity, especially concerned with social improvement, social justice, peace and reconciliation.

Of course, much has changed across the decades since the 1920s. The Welfare State has come into being, with all its attendant benefits – and challenges. Philanthropy is no longer just local, but also national and global. Cadburys became a multinational firm, and is now owned by an American company. The Barrow Cadbury Trust has diversified its investments, and is no longer based in Birmingham. But it is still chaired by a member of the Cadbury family, and remains true to the original vision of its founders. As these timely and enthralling pages serve to show, 'the chocolate conscience' is still hard at work – and it still has plenty to do.

Introduction
Barrow Cadbury's Cupboard

As a very old man, Barrow Cadbury frequently invited those seeking his help to visit him at home in Birmingham. He enjoyed hearing about the various initiatives that his Trust might support, particularly if the cause was one with which his wife Geraldine had been involved. During the 1920s and 30s the Trust had funded the building of open-air schools, the Juvenile Court in Birmingham and several hostels for young offenders. Having discussed a request for help, Barrow would more often than not get up from his chair, go to a drawer in the polished wood cupboard, which also served as a safe, and take out a cheque book. He would move to his desk, on which were neat piles of papers mostly concerned with scores of charitable projects. In his elegant, precise handwriting – it remained firm and virtually unchanged well into his nineties – he would write out a cheque on behalf of the Barrow & Geraldine S Cadbury Trust.

Geraldine (née Southall) Cadbury DBE (1865–1941).

Opposite *Barrow Cadbury (1862–1958).*

He and his wife had set up the Trust in 1920, drawing its income from shares in the company of Cadbury Brothers Limited, of which he was chairman from 1922 to 1932. After Geraldine's death in 1941 at the age of 76, the Trust became as much a memorial to her as it was an expression of Barrow's deep Quaker convictions. He died in 1958, when he was 95.

Half a century later an approach to their Trust would be dealt with rather differently. The first step might be to consult the website of what is now called simply the Barrow Cadbury Trust. Then the enquiry might progress to an email to the Trust's London office. Guidance would be given by one of the Trust's professional staff. If responses were encouraging, the application would be referred to one of the regular meetings of the board of trustees, which is still chaired by a member of the Cadbury family. In due course it might feature, along with other projects, in the Trust's annual report.

Bull Street, Birmingham, showing the tea, coffee and cocoa shop established by John Cadbury in 1824, next to the drapers opened by his father, Richard Tapper Cadbury, in 1794.

The transformation of the Barrow Cadbury Trust mirrors to some extent the growth of the firm of Cadbury, from a modest shop in Bull Street, Birmingham, to a multi-national enterprise. While there are continuities in its story, and many of the underlying ideals and objectives are constant, it has needed to evolve. That adaptability helps to explain why it is still relevant and effective today.

When seen in the context of changing attitudes to personal philanthropy, the history of the Trust is particularly interesting and instructive. During the early 1900s there was intense and often heated debate about the role of government and the place of private charitable giving. Attitudes to the relationship between the statutory and voluntary sectors changed profoundly in the first decade of the last century and again after 1945, with the arrival of the Welfare State. First Barrow, and then Geraldine, Cadbury were part of those debates, with their son Paul Cadbury engaging equally energetically after the Second World War. The significance of these changes of context to the work of the Trust is the subject of later chapters and recurs throughout the book. The debate is very much alive today, although often conducted by politicians who may not always be aware of history or precedent. They might act more wisely if they were.

The development of the Trust was in part a response to those external changes. It is also the story of a very successful Quaker family who were deeply concerned for the welfare of their fellow men and wanted to see a more just society. Previous accounts of their philanthropy tended towards the pious and were written without much concern for the wider picture. Somehow Barrow Cadbury becomes more humane when his explosive temper is acknowledged. Geraldine's kindness towards young offenders was exceptional and touching, but she herself acknowledged that she was not one "to suffer fools gladly", and she was ready when necessary to make her dissatisfaction clear if an official or a probation officer did not come up to the mark. Some of Barrow's initiatives were misconceived and occasionally his tendency to see the best in everyone left him deluded, as happened when he joined a peace delegation to Germany in 1914.

None of that detracts from their achievements. No one reading about Barrow and Geraldine Cadbury, or about Paul Cadbury, can fail to be struck by how much energy and originality they brought to their various charitable initiatives and by the influence they had on government thinking, particularly over attitudes to child delinquency. The people of Birmingham, and society more widely, were the better for the Cadburys' work and generosity. They, and the Barrow Cadbury Trust, have been a powerful force for good.

Chapter 1
The Cadburys, The Southalls and The Quaker Inheritance

When Barrow Cadbury was born on 27 September 1862, the business in which his family was engaged was precarious and its future uncertain. His great-grandfather Richard Tapper Cadbury had moved from Exeter to Birmingham in 1794 and set up a drapery business in Bull Street. He became a much respected member of the Birmingham business community, serving on the Board of the General Hospital and as an overseer of the poor.

Richard's son John established himself as a tea, coffee and cocoa dealer in 1824, taking premises next to the drapers run by his father. Most of his customers were fellow Quakers or Unitarians. He also looked to a fellow Quaker and grocer, Joseph Rowntree (1836–1925), to take on his son George as an apprentice. The experience was to be formative, not just in terms of teaching him sound business practice, but also in introducing him to a family who were to be both friends and rivals, and who would provide a model for the Cadbury charitable trusts. By 1854 the firm was sufficiently well-established to be able to open premises in London, and was appointed Cocoa Manufacturers to Queen Victoria. But selling luxury goods at a time of economic depression was hard, and there was illness in the Cadbury family. The outlook was so unpromising that in 1861 John Cadbury was forced to withdraw from the business. His two sons, George and Richard, contemplated giving up altogether, with the former planning to go to Ceylon as a tea planter and the latter thinking of training as a surveyor. They struggled on, not allowing the poor returns to discourage them from steadily improving the quality of their chocolate, from making the wrappers more colourful, and from employing travellers whose job it was to market their products throughout the country.

John Cadbury (1801–89) by B Fleetwood-Walker.

Opposite *Barrow Cadbury with his father, Richard Cadbury (1835–99), c.1866.*

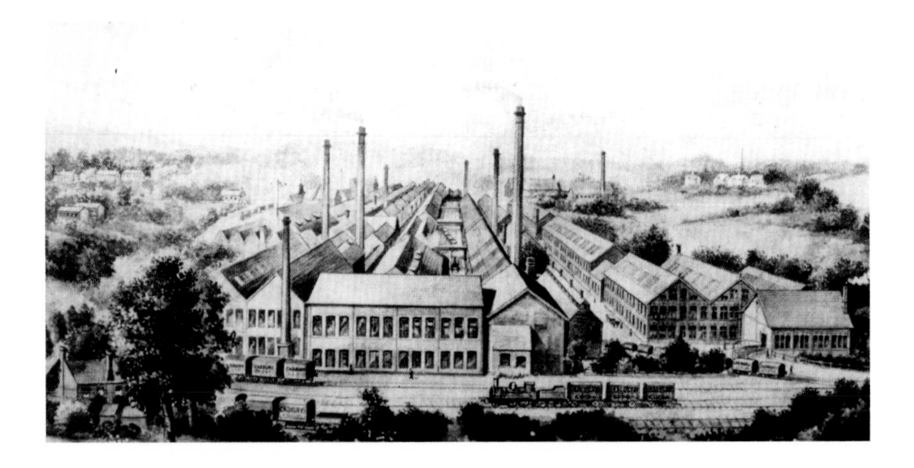

The Bournville Factory, built by George and Richard Cadbury in 1879.

The turning point came in 1870 with the advent of the Franco-Prussian War, just when the firm was beginning to reap the benefits of improved technology and imaginative advertising.

French, and particularly Parisian, chocolate had previously dominated the luxury market. The siege of Paris from September 1870 to January 1871 had shattered the city, wrecked its credit system and left it in no state to retain its export markets. The Cadbury brothers were perfectly poised to seize the opportunity. By 1879 the firm was employing 300 workers, and the same year George and Richard Cadbury began building a new works four miles from the centre of Birmingham, on a site south of the city and well served by both the railway and canals. They chose to call the new factory Bournville, combining the name of the nearby Bourn brook with the French-sounding *ville* to appeal to customers who had previously favoured Continental chocolates. By 1889 the number of employees had grown to 1,200, and by the end of the century there were over 2,700 workers at Bournville.

The choice and design of Bournville was influenced by more than business considerations. After he had left the firm, John Cadbury had devoted himself to improving the conditions of the Birmingham poor. He was involved with the Society for the Relief of Infirm and Aged Women, supported the Blind Asylum and campaigned vigorously against the employment of small boys to climb and sweep chimneys. His son George's response to the social problems of Birmingham was more fundamental. He wanted to create his own community around a reliable source of employment, and with provisions for his employees that looked after their needs from cradle to grave. There were plenty of precedents to influence him, including Robert Owen's New Lanark Mills of 1800, in Scotland, and the Greg family's mill and village at

Quarry Bank near Styal in Cheshire. Yet the new Cadbury factory went far beyond these early nineteenth-century experiments. Workers were provided with a relatively safe place of work, with dining-rooms, a sports ground, medical care and, in due course, with adult education. It was paternalistic, socially inhibiting and influenced by business interests; but it was appreciated by those prepared to embrace the security it offered. Meanwhile, the company continued to prosper, and on the death of Richard Cadbury – Barrow's father – in 1899, Cadbury Bros became a private limited company, with George Cadbury as its first chairman.

The Southall family were also Birmingham Quakers. Alfred Southall, Geraldine's father, was a chemist and, like the Cadburys, had premises in Bull Street. His wife Anna was from the Grubb family of Irish Quakers. They had met at the Quaker Meeting House in Bull Street, and were married in 1864. Anna Southall's views were radical, and she was an outspoken advocate of women's suffrage. On at least one occasion she attended a meeting to discuss Irish Home Rule, and before a hostile audience spoke powerfully about poverty and famine in Ireland. She became president of the Friends' Reading Society and lectured widely in Birmingham on public health and the care of young children.

Four generations: left to right, *Geraldine Cadbury holding her granddaughter, Catherine (b. 1920), with her son, Paul (1895–1984) and her father, Alfred Southall (1838–1931).*

In 1865, at the time that the Cadburys were thinking of moving their works out of the centre of Birmingham, Alfred Southall diversified his business and set up a coffee house. In a typically Quaker way, the venture was partly to further temperance but also to exploit a business opportunity. The family prospered and moved to a substantial house in the fashionable suburb of Edgbaston. Geraldine was born on 29 June 1865, the eldest of nine children, and sent first to the Edgbaston High School for Girls – where she was a contemporary of Joseph Chamberlain's daughters – and then to the Mount School in York, the leading Quaker boarding school for girls. Her education was cut short however when she had to return home to help look after her young siblings during the steady decline in her mother's health. She contemplated a university education, but instead was given the post of manager at her father's works, supervising around 100 female workers. Geraldine met the young Barrow Cadbury at the Bull Street Meeting House – they became engaged in 1890, after a courtship of a year or so, and were married on 8 September 1891. It was to prove an exceptionally happy and fruitful marriage.

Barrow and Geraldine Cadbury in 1891.

By the middle years of the nineteenth century, Quakers were beginning to win for themselves a prominent and respected place in national life. Their central beliefs, articulated simply and powerfully by their founder George Fox (1624–91), did not alter. The Society of Friends believed that God spoke to the individual and that spiritual truth was to be found in the heart, not in the trappings of organised religion. All men were equal before God, and consequently respect for worldly status and authority was misplaced, to the extent that it was wrong to doff one's hat as a mark of deference. The taking of oaths implied that at other times the individual was expected to act untruthfully – and this was morally unacceptable.

Barrow and Geraldine Cadbury's wedding, 8 September 1891.

In 1649 this attitude landed Fox in jail, and many of his followers readily followed his example, welcoming the abusive name 'Quakers' as a badge of uncompromising principle. The Society was adamantly opposed to slavery, social injustice and excessive personal indulgence – whether in clothes, food or drink – and no less insistent that Friends should marry other Friends. It was their standards of integrity and discipline that made them trusted as bankers and businessmen. Their mutual support and interdependence enabled them to establish a national and international business network, not least with Quakers in the British colonies in North America and later in the United States. Non-conformity was not only fundamental to their religious beliefs but was also an attitude of mind. It helps to explain why they were always ready to innovate, whether in the fields of industrial processes, entrepreneurship or social welfare.

Even in the middle of the nineteenth century the heroic struggles, suffering and sacrifices of the seventeenth and eighteenth centuries were not forgotten. They would always set a standard for moral integrity which was applied by Quakers to religious, social, commercial and political life. Acceptance of the Quakers reflected a sometimes grudging toleration of their beliefs and – in a peculiarly British way – a willingness to embrace their business success and the fortunes that went with it. In the great cities of the Midlands and the north of England the Quakers held positions of unquestioned power and influence.

Elizabeth Fry (1780–1845), English prison reformer and Quaker philanthropist. Since 2001 she has been depicted on the Bank of England £5 note.

The process of assimilation is illustrated by the lives of the Pease family of Darlington in County Durham. Edward Pease (1767–1858) was a successful industrialist, a founder of the Peace Society and a supporter of the Anti-Slavery Society. It was his support for George Stephenson that made possible the building of the world's first railway, from Stockton to Darlington. His son Joseph Pease (1799–1872) became a hugely successful owner of collieries, quarries and cotton mills in the Durham area, and by the time of his death was employing 10,000 workmen. His family were Quakers and his wife was a Gurney, so he was related by marriage to Elizabeth Fry (*née* Gurney, 1780–1845), who was described by Geraldine Cadbury as her "patron saint". Following the passing of the Reform Act of 1832 Joseph Pease was elected to Parliament as the first Quaker MP, representing South Durham, and was eventually allowed to take his seat in 1833 on giving an affirmation, rather than swearing an oath. He was a champion of social and political reform in the House of Commons, where he spoke without using titles, refused to remove his hat and always wore Quaker dress. As so often with Quaker families, there was a connection by marriage with the Cadburys, in this case through Paul's wife Rachel Wilson, who had inherited some of her determination and competence from her Pease forebears.

The barriers to a full public life were dismantled only gradually. Although religious disqualifications from holding public office were removed in 1828, dissenters were still subject to Church Rates until 1867, and it was not until 1871 that all posts and prizes at the older universities were open to them. At a time when the universities were supine and unreformed, this may not have been a disadvantage. As Sir Adrian Cadbury (who rowed for Cambridge University) ironically observed of his early nineteenth-century forebears, "It did us absolutely no harm not being in dead-beat universities like Cambridge." For Quakers such as Barrow and Geraldine Cadbury, born in the 1860s, the sense of exclusivity, if not exclusion, was remembered with pride. One of the reasons why they and many other Quakers remained so firmly committed to confronting the *status quo* was that they were non-conformists, and resolutely so.

In the nineteenth century the Society of Friends made assimilation easier by modifying and reforming some of the more eccentric practices that had been passed down by their seventeenth-century founders, in particular George Fox. One of the more serious obstacles to wider acceptance was the disowning of those who chose to marry outside the Society. For Barrow and Geraldine this was not an issue, but it was for many others.

In 1859 John Stephenson Rowntree published his *Quakerism: past and present*, which argued that some Quaker discipline was excessive and the Society would be the stronger for "more knowledge of the wider world". There was acceptance of the fashionable entertainment of theatres and dances by the so-called 'gay' Friends, although many Quakers, including Elizabeth Fry, preferred to remain one of the 'plain' Friends.

Faced with these choices about how best to express their Quaker beliefs, Barrow and Geraldine Cadbury seem to have opted for a middle course. They remained staunch supporters of the temperance movement, gave generously to Quaker Meeting Houses throughout the country and were strict in their observance of the Sabbath. Barrow never questioned the routine of daily worship at the Bournville factory.

Geraldine's parents in particular adopted a much less rigid interpretation of Quaker religious practice, and this in time influenced Barrow. Her family were never sympathetic to the idea that a Quaker way of life should mean detachment from the political and social issues of the day. One perhaps surprising expression of their open-mindedness is that Cardinal Newman was a regular visitor to Alfred Southall's chemist shop in Bull Street, which supplied his preferred formulation of incense for use at the Roman Catholic Birmingham Oratory. In 1890 both Geraldine and her mother went to pay their respects at the Cardinal's lying-in-repose, and Geraldine returned a second time with her younger sister Kathleen. The Cardinal's great hymn, *Lead, Kindly Light*, remained one of her favourites, and she kept a picture of him on her desk until she died.

For many Quakers a love of art was a sign of frivolity and worldliness. This was not the case with either the Cadburys or the Southalls. Richard Cadbury was a talented amateur artist and used his watercolours of the family in some of his chocolate-box designs. The picture of a small boy holding a model yacht is almost certainly a portrait of his son Barrow.

In later life Richard was enthralled by the archaeology of ancient Egypt, contributing to the cost of excavations there, and he died from an illness contracted during an extended tour of the sites along the Nile. During their married life, Barrow and Geraldine were enthusiastic visitors to the great museums of Europe and their Trust made a regular annual subscription to the Birmingham Art Gallery. Geraldine's knowledge of art was the result of extensive reading and she shared it enthusiastically with her husband.

Barrow and Geraldine Cadbury on holiday in Egypt with their daughters, Dorothy and Cherry.

Barrow and Geraldine Cadbury in June 1892.

Both of them were similarly relaxed about dress. Barrow usually wore a sombre suit, but that was expected of any successful Birmingham businessman. Geraldine wore elegant clothes, and Barrow gave her presents of jewellery. In 1909, when Barrow was part of a delegation of bishops and community leaders sent to Germany in an attempt to allay mutual suspicions and increasing militarism, he wrote to tell Geraldine that "there was a clerical atmosphere at Charing Cross, and gaiters and clerical ties in some evidence." This prompted him to sport a more than usually bright tie.

To assume that the way the Cadbury family ran their business was entirely shaped by their Quaker convictions would be an over-simplification. Their photograph albums have pictures of the great social reformers, thinkers and writers of the Victorian age, including Charles Dickens, Thomas Carlyle and – most important of all – John Ruskin. It was not Ruskin the art critic and champion of Turner who first attracted them, but Ruskin the author of books on the state of industry and employment, which were vilified in the conservative press. His four essays, published as *Unto This Last* in 1860, set out the case for a better way of ordering society and a more responsible attitude to the generation of wealth, in prose that was brilliant and passionate. He wrote of the "balances of justice" and then explained that he meant "the term justice, to include affection – such affection as one man *owes* to another. All right relations between master and operative, and all their best interests, ultimately depend on these." There is a passage in *Unto This Last* on schools and prisons that might have been written many years later by Geraldine Cadbury:

> *If you examine into the history of rogues, you will find they are as truly manufactured articles as anything else, and it is just because our present system of political economy gives so large a stimulus to that manufacture that you may know it to be a false one. We had better seek for a system which will develop honest men, than for one which will deal cunningly with vagabonds. Let us reform our schools, and you shall find little reform needed in our prisons.*

Not only did Ruskin's portrait find a place in the Cadbury household, but what eventually was called the Bournville School of Arts and Crafts was originally named Ruskin Hall. As an old lady, Geraldine recalled what she had learnt from Ruskin. When she was asked in 1937 to present the Gold Medal and Awards for Landscape Art to the Birmingham Art School, she opened her speech by saying that, "I know nothing about modern landscape art. I was brought up in the days of Ruskin ... He taught us that 'the two great ends of landscape painting are the representation of facts and thoughts, and that the truth of nature is not to be discovered by the uneducated senses'." What she did not tell her audience was that as a girl she was so in thrall to Ruskin that, while on a family holiday in the Lake District, she had attempted to visit him at Brantwood, his home on Coniston Water. She had knocked on his door but then, overcome with shyness, had hurried away.

Ruskin not only helped to shape Geraldine's thinking on social issues. His advocacy of honest craftsmanship and the use of fine materials seems to have influenced her many building projects and the care she took over the design and choice of tiles and textiles.

In the essentials of their Quaker beliefs, Barrow and Geraldine never wavered. Their letters were often colourful and amusing, but then a note of Quaker sobriety would suddenly break in. Another Barrow letter of 1909 abruptly reverts to the Quaker pattern of antiquated speech and ends by referring to Geraldine as "the dearest, sweetest girl in the world, to whom I owe so much, whom I love so much, and to whom I may joyfully write as Thy husband *Barrow Cadbury*."

A century later his great-granddaughter Anna Southall explained that even when members of the family choose not to be formal members of the Society of Friends, the fundamental beliefs and values of the Quakers are inescapably in their blood. A very similar point was made by Sir Adrian Cadbury, a former chairman of the family business:

> *It's the belief that the light is in everyone; every individual has something to offer. And, if you look at it from a business point of view, our job is to enable people, individuals, to make the most of their abilities and talents. It's the belief in the importance of the individual; and therefore the distinction between men and women is irrelevant.*

Those values were, and are, personal. They also continue to permeate the work of the Barrow Cadbury Trust.

John Ruskin (1819–1900) in his study at Brantwood on Coniston Water, Cumberland, by WG Collingwood.

Chapter 2
A Crisis in Philanthropy

In 1890, the year that Barrow became engaged to Geraldine, there was acute poverty and distress in Birmingham. There was also a growing awareness that although Britain was enjoying unrivalled prosperity, its treatment of the poor was often brutal and demeaning. Education for most of the population lagged behind what was practiced in other European countries. Improvements to public health in the great industrial cities had been slow and grudging. The Cadbury family's response to what became an acrimonious debate about the role of the State and the place of private philanthropy was typically non-conformist.

In the 1850s there was widespread reaction against the more centralised approach to public health that had been championed by Lord Shaftesbury and Edwin Chadwick, the secretary of the Poor Law Commission, and which had culminated in the Public Health Act of 1848. Those who opposed the interference by central government in issues of social welfare were motivated partly by self-interest – they resented increases in rates and taxation – and partly by the economic theories of Jeremy Bentham and his disciples, who advocated minimal state intervention in the lives of ordinary citizens. In the mid-nineteenth century these reactionary views prevailed, and in 1858 the Board of Health was abolished. The forces of dirt and decentralisation appeared to have triumphed.

An increasingly harsh attitude to pauperism was buttressed by philosophical arguments put forward by the Charity Organisation Society. Its name may suggest an enlightened restructuring of charitable provision, and that indeed was partly why it was founded in 1869. Its initial aims were straightforward and admirable: to discourage indiscriminate almsgiving to the poor and encourage self-reliance. The Society attracted generous donations from John Ruskin and the active support of Octavia Hill, whose housing work for the poor in London was strongly influenced by its principles. The council of the Society was, however, a hotbed of personal rivalries and acrimonious disagreements. Its attitudes to pauperism became increasingly doctrinaire, authoritarian and lacking in kindness and understanding. The Society vigorously promoted the view that it was the feebleness and indolence of the poor that was the cause of their distress, and that well-intentioned but misdirected philanthropy was encouraging, not alleviating, pauperism. Human weakness, not the organisation of society, was at fault and the Poor Law was attacked as an inducement to dependence and idleness. In the eyes of the Charity Organisation Society there might be a place for charity and mutual aid directed at the so-called 'deserving' poor, but the well-being of most of society derived from the urge towards self-help.

The policies of the Charity Organisation Society now seem deluded and heartless, but they were passionately held and widely promulgated. For example, the Society strongly opposed schemes to provide children from poor families with free school meals, because they believed that such initiatives amounted to misguided almsgiving and encouraged parental neglect. These views were vigorously expressed in a Society pamphlet of 1889, entitled *The Feeding of School Children.*

Barrow and Geraldine Cadbury were drawn into these debates about the alleviation of poverty, and they witnessed at first hand the appalling conditions of the Birmingham poor. In January 1891, shortly after their engagement, Geraldine wrote to Barrow:

> *Yesterday afternoon early there was a great crowd round the Charity Organization Rooms in Broad Street – they say there is a crowd there every day now. When I was coming up Broad Street at 5 p.m., the crowd seemed just as great, but I found they had admitted the last applicant for the day, and the police were trying to disperse the rest. There was really an awful look on the faces of some as they begged to be allowed to go in, and perhaps the saddest part was these looked the most respectable. There is indeed great distress here this winter.*

'Back to Backs' housing in central Birmingham, recorded in the Graphic *magazine in 1876, shortly before many were condemned for demolition under the Artisans' Dwelling Act.*

She went on to describe a visit to a young mother unable to look after a large family:

> *To-day I went to the poor woman in Staniforth Street to whom I sent on Sunday one of your notes. For several weeks her husband has brought her ten shillings, and a daughter who is in my class six shillings. Two wild sons spend what they get, though the mother said pitifully, "The wildest is the best of the two; he asks me how I am and wishes he could do something for me; the other does not even ask how I feel!" She was in bed with four children to look after – one a baby, and the other three bad with whooping cough, and she hoped a neighbour might look in to see to her a bit! The one bright spot seemed to be the daily visits of a Sunday-school girl of mine who had made her broth, seen to the children a little, read the Bible to her, and prayed with her.*

A very different response to the problems of poverty had been demonstrated to Barrow by his uncle George Cadbury. Indeed, Barrow seems to have based his and Geraldine's approach to philanthropy on the example of George Cadbury, as well as on that of Joseph Rowntree and his son Seebohm. Their Quaker beliefs underpinned these other influences. They accepted that there might occasionally be a place for relieving temporary distress, but they were more concerned to address the fundamental causes of poverty. In their pursuit of a better and healthier society the Cadbury family set out to create a model of enlightened employment, whilst also arguing strongly for effective intervention from both central and local government.

Bust of George Cadbury (1839–1922) by Francis Wood, erected outside the Friends' Meeting House at Bournville in 1924.

David Owen, the historian of English philanthropy, has written that "George Cadbury's whole career was a venture in philanthropy" and that his theory and practice provided a model for the nephew who was to become a trusted business partner. Philanthropy, for George Cadbury, began at home, with his attitude to inherited wealth. His children accepted that the profits from the business should be directed to the Bournville Village Trust and not to them. Personal wealth, George believed, was "more a curse than a blessing to the families of those who possess it". He supported graduated income tax enthusiastically, and advocated stiff death duties as a means of returning to the nation the wealth which ought to have been used to improve society. He himself gave away almost all his income, partly

Early housing schemes built at Bournville for Cadbury employees and other local people, c.*1910.*

on the grounds that "my children will be all the better for being deprived of this money."

At the time when the Charity Organisation Society was still adhering rigidly to its policy of resistance to welfare legislation, George Cadbury was very publicly supporting campaigns for old age pensions and against sweated labour. The Liberal government which came to power in 1906 with a large majority provoked hostility from industrialists and landowners for its advocacy of higher income tax, a state pension for those at the age of 70 and over, and – to achieve these aims – a curb on the power of the House of Lords. On all these issues, the Cadburys were on the side of reform. George's influence was an important factor in the passing of the Old Age Pensions Act in 1908.

Few would now dispute that history has proved the advocates of reform right. For the Cadbury family, a better, fairer society could only be achieved by a combination of state action and individual effort. With their increasing wealth and influence they were in a position to encourage both.

Barrow Cadbury's character, both as a businessman and as a public benefactor, was shaped by two crucial experiences in his personal life. One was his unhappy childhood, the other his long and fulfilling marriage to Geraldine. His loneliness as a child made him reserved and undemonstrative as an adult, except when the explosive temper he had inherited from his father got the better of him. He was capable of tearing up sample designs for packaging which dissatisfied him. Under Geraldine's influence, however, Barrow readily threw his influence and wealth behind increasingly radical and influential experiments in social improvement. Many of the initiatives that were to be of lasting significance were an expression of his deep affection for his wife and his confidence that her often pioneering solutions to social problems deserved the very substantial financial support that he was in a position to give them.

Although Geraldine may often have taken the initiative, the tragedy in Barrow's own early life may also have made him sympathetic to the plight of deprived children. His mother Elizabeth died in 1868, when she was just 30 and Barrow was six. He was thought of as a sickly child, although his illnesses might partly have been an expression of insecurity. His father Richard married again and had four daughters with his second wife, Emma. At the age of 11, Barrow was sent to Germany to attend a *Realschule* (or state elementary school) in Stuttgart. In many ways it was a curious choice of education for a young Quaker. Instead of games the boys were drilled on a parade ground and had military training, with short iron rods substituting for muskets. Much later in life he noted with satisfaction that "one good result of the war" was the abolition in 1948 of caning in German schools. On a more positive note, he later valued the religious tolerance that he learnt in Germany, from attending Church of England services on Sunday mornings and Lutheran ones in the afternoons.

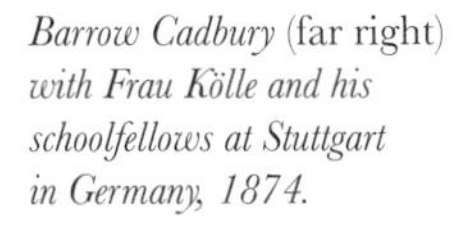

Barrow Cadbury (far right) *with Frau Kölle and his schoolfellows at Stuttgart in Germany, 1874.*

Barrow and Geraldine Cadbury with their children in 1908: Paul (far left), *Dorothy* (standing) *and Cherry* (seated on her mother's lap).

Geraldine's childhood was, by comparison, full of the affection of a large family, of which she was the eldest. Helping to look after her younger siblings was a central part of her early life. Her father expected his children to follow his Spartan example: no curtains or carpets in bedrooms, and certainly no overcoats. Her mother involved her in helping at the Crowley Orphanage and the Adult School Women's Class, but also encouraged her skills as a needlewoman and botanical illustrator. Geraldine developed strong convictions and a willingness to express herself in a forthright way, whilst maintaining an easy, outgoing manner. These qualities were to be a valuable foil to Barrow's diffidence and reserve.

In the early years of their marriage the couple were not particularly rich, living happily and simply in a modest semi-detached house in Highfield Road, Birmingham. Their daughter Dorothy was born in 1892, a son Paul in 1895, and in 1900 they had a third child, also named Geraldine but known in the family as Cherry. Barrow's father died in 1899 and two years later the young family moved into Southfield, a substantial house in Wheeleys Road, Edgbaston. Their new home reflected Barrow's rising position in the family business. Southfield had formerly belonged to Joseph Sturge, champion of the Adult School movement in the 1840s and a Quaker who was a passionate opponent of slavery. These were causes which Barrow and Geraldine readily espoused.

As an old man Barrow wrote an essay for his family on marriage and home-building, passing on some of his experiences of 50 years of happy companionship. Towards the end he noted:

> *Giving should not be forgotten. If you two can put aside annually (month by month) the sum you feel it right to set aside for giving, you will find much joy in planning together how it should be used through the year. Many lose this joy by waiting until they can give larger sums; there is an equal joy in the little gift which goes with love behind it. Let your children share where they can in your counsels; it will help them when they take your places.*

On his father's death, Barrow became a wealthy man. The following year, in 1900, the company of Cadbury Bros Limited was formed, making Barrow a major shareholder. He became one of the four newly appointed managing directors, on a substantial salary. His and Geraldine's giving came partly from this salary and increasingly from the income drawn from his shares. In due course a large part of these shares in the business were to be put into a charitable trust which would fund causes that he and Geraldine had long supported.

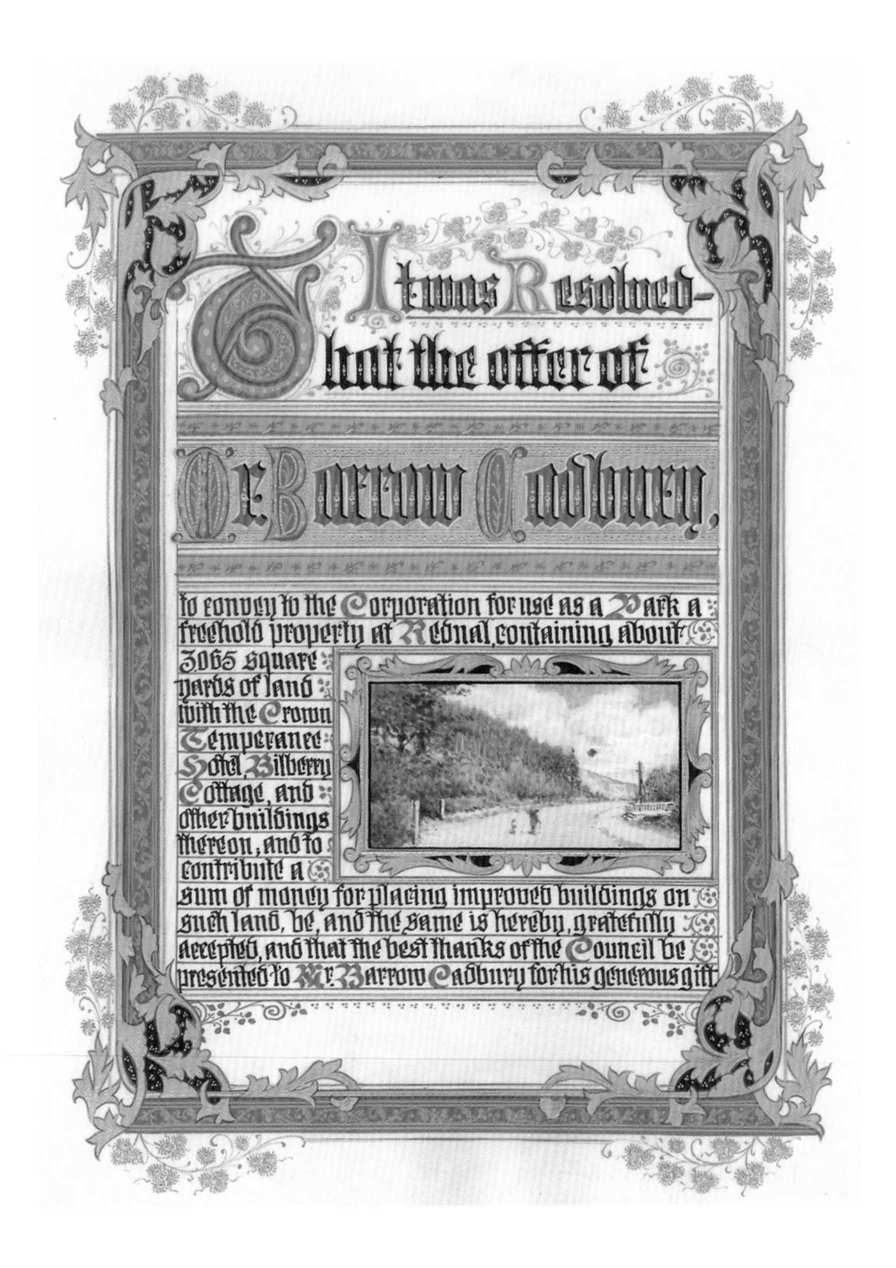

It was Resolved—
That the offer of
Mr. Barrow Cadbury,
to convey to the Corporation for use as a Park a freehold property at Rednal, containing about 3065 square yards of land with the Crown Temperance Hotel, Bilberry Cottage, and other buildings thereon, and to contribute a sum of money for placing improved buildings on such land, be, and the same is hereby, gratefully accepted, and that the best thanks of the Council be presented to Mr. Barrow Cadbury for his generous gift.

Illuminated deed commissioned by Birmingham City Council to record Barrow Cadbury's gift to the city of 3,065 square yards of the Lickey Hills, with the Crown Temperance Hotel, on 7 July 1903. The land is now one of Birmingham's most popular country parks.

Much of their early giving was to institutes and other Quaker activities to which Barrow's father had contributed. Barrow gave generously to the Friends' Institute in Moseley Road, Birmingham, which was nearing completion at the time of Richard Cadbury's death. In 1902 Barrow and Geraldine built a new institute at Greet, a suburb of Birmingham, which included an adult school, a Sunday school and facilities for a women's meeting. Two years later they provided the Greet Nursery School, the first in the city and an early example of Geraldine's personal involvement in the design of both the building and its equipment. The windows were large and set low down so that children could see the garden, and special child-sized chairs and tables were commissioned. Pupils attending the school were encouraged to tend the plants in the windowboxes and to look after the pet doves, rabbits, hens and parrot.

Adult education was a continuing preoccupation for Barrow and Geraldine. On the death of his stepmother Emma in 1907, Barrow purchased from her trustees the house which his father had designed for himself in 1894. Built on a grand scale and furnished with antiques, plentiful stuffed birds and bearskins, Uffculme was not associated by Barrow with happy childhood memories and in any case he and Geraldine preferred to live in a simpler, less pretentious style. They agreed therefore that the house should become a residential Adult School Hostel. During the First World War it was used briefly as a home for children evacuated from Birmingham, as a distributing centre for Belgian refugees, and then, in 1916, as a hospital for wounded soldiers run by the Friends' Ambulance Unit (*see* page 60). After the war the house and grounds were given to the City of Birmingham, with the adjoining land at Highbury, once the home of Joseph Chamberlain. The combination of education and public recreation provided at Uffculme reflected Barrow and Geraldine's growing conviction that addressing the root cause of social problems was essential. In this belief they were building on what George and Richard Cadbury had set out to provide at Bournville.

Uffculme House, built by Richard Cadbury in 1894 and donated by Barrow Cadbury as a hostel for Belgian refugees and a hospital for the Friends' Ambulance Unit during the First World War.

Barrow and Geraldine's generosity might well have been concentrated on comfortable projects of this sort. But in the early 1900s both became increasingly committed to addressing far more intractable social issues and specifically to the provision of juvenile courts and to penal reform. Here they began to break new ground and move beyond the more conventional expressions of Victorian philanthropy. They were part of a new, brave and humane way of dealing with juvenile crime that was initiated in Birmingham – ahead of other British cities – and made possible by their gifts to the city. These provisions were to have considerable national significance, and meanwhile both Barrow and Geraldine became determined that a major part of their charitable giving was to be directed towards the pursuit of social justice.

Barrow Cadbury and Geraldine's father, Alfred Southall, both became magistrates in 1906, at a time when the way in which the courts dealt with children was being reviewed, a process that was long overdue. The previous year Courtenay Lord, who had recently been appointed a Visiting Justice, was concerned to find that young offenders were being sent to Birmingham's Winson Green Prison, where they mixed with adult prisoners or were left in their cells with nothing to do. Taking as his model a widely admired and publicised American Children's Court in Denver, Colorado, Lord put forward a scheme to his fellow magistrates "for dealing with children and youthful offenders". The outcome was agreement from the Birmingham City Council's Watch Committee that children should be tried separately from adults in a newly created Children's Court. They would enter court by a different door, cases of juvenile crime would be heard before the main business of the day, and no children were to be put in the dock.

At the invitation of Mrs Dickinson Sturge, a Quaker who regularly visited young girls who were due to appear in court, Geraldine Cadbury undertook to act as an observer of first-time offenders, in all but name becoming an unpaid probation officer. As a result she was, from the very beginning, part of an enlightened experiment in the way in which juvenile courts were to be run in Birmingham. It was an experience that was to change her life and give her a leading role, first regionally and then nationally, in transforming the way in which society regarded delinquent children.

After an experimental year, the Children's Court was approved formally by the Home Office. There was agreement "that a regular rota of magistrates willing to devote their time to this court should be arranged in order to ensure a regularity of procedure". By 1907 the Home Office was advocating

The Children's Remand Home in Moseley Road, Birmingham, built by Barrow and Geraldine Cadbury in 1910 and photographed – unused and boarded up – in 2010.

that similar courts should be established in other cities, and in the same year salaried probation officers were given statutory recognition via the Probation Act. In 1908 the Children's Act made provision for children's courts nationwide, using the Birmingham experiment – acknowledged, after two years, to be a success – as a model.

The principle that children who had fallen foul of the law should be treated differently from adults had therefore been established. But if the change in approach was to be consolidated, proper provision for the detention of young people was urgently needed. Barrow and Geraldine saw this as an opportunity to take a leading role and in November 1909 wrote to the Birmingham Watch Committee, "offering to furnish and equip a house suitable for a Remand Home, where children brought before the magistrates might be sent". Not only did they commission a new building in Moseley Road, Birmingham – the first purpose-built remand home in the country and which opened on 9 December 1910 – but Geraldine personally supervised its furnishing and decoration. Thereafter she concerned herself as much with the case histories of the children who attended the Birmingham Children's Remand Home as she did with its bricks and mortar, keeping a card index recording the personal details of almost every child who passed through the premises. The magistrates dealing with offenders would be given a detailed brief by Geraldine on those brought before them, which also often explained the circumstances that had led the child into criminality.

Paul Cadbury at Cropwood during his fresh-air cure, with his sisters Cherry and Dorothy, c.*1906–7.*

What prompted Geraldine Cadbury to embark on this influential initiative? Many years later, in 1938, she published a book which she called *Young Offenders Yesterday and Today*. Her usually reliable biographer Janet Whitney thought it unsatisfactory and concluded that "expression in the written word was not her *forte*". The book is, however, full of humanity and good sense, is carefully researched, touching, and reveals much about Geraldine herself. Perhaps the most impressive feature of it is the absence of too emotional a response to the problems of deprived children, an issue which she approached with realism and a firm belief in the value of practical schemes for social improvement.

What is very evident in her book is the extent to which Geraldine saw herself in a long line of Quaker advocates of judicial reform. She wrote particularly admiringly of Peter Bedford, who lived in Spitalfields in east London and in 1815 formed a society "for investigating the causes of the alarming increase in juvenile delinquency in the metropolis". He had been profoundly disturbed by the Old Bailey sessions on a single day in February 1814, when five children were condemned to death, including boys of eight, nine and eleven, the latter for stealing a pair of shoes. Geraldine contrasted their treatment with the aims of the farm colony set up at Stretton-on-Dunsmore in Warwickshire in 1818, which hired out boys from county gaols to work on local farms, with the aim of reforming rather than punishing them. Another constant inspiration to her was the prison reformer Elizabeth Fry.

Those admired by Geraldine were not exclusively Quakers. She praised Sir William Harcourt for his enlightened and determined action while Home Secretary from 1880–85, and particularly for his willingness to confront the highest ranks of the establishment. When Queen Victoria pronounced herself "disturbed by what she felt was his undue tenderness to offenders," his reply was robust. Writing in September 1880 – and quoted by Geraldine – Harcourt told the Queen that in many cases the offences committed by children were trifling, citing a sentence of twelve years' imprisonment for "damaging grass by running about in two fields" and the long prison terms given to boys of 12 and 13 for bathing in a canal.

Geraldine's vigorous non-conformity is evident in her quotations from letters written from Balmoral by the Queen's private secretary, in which he tells Harcourt that "H.M. was really interested in all you said about youthful criminals. She would like to whip them, but it seems that that cannot be done." To this Geraldine noted, "One wonders what punishments were used in the royal nursery!"

At the time Geraldine was beginning to involve herself in the juvenile court system, the health of her son Paul was steadily deteriorating. His illness was thought to be tuberculosis and an eminent doctor, Sir Thomas Barlow, was consulted. He recommended taking Paul out of school, educating him at home in the country and ensuring that he had plenty of good food and fresh air. From 1907 the family spent increasing amounts of time at Cropwood, a house they had built for themselves in the Lickey Hills, south-west of Birmingham, where Paul's bedroom had one wall that was completely open to the outside elements. Both Barrow and Geraldine were energetic walkers, and the regime advocated for Paul also suited them. His younger sister Cherry, who sometimes slept on the veranda, recalled in 1994 that "my mother crocheted little hoods for us all so we didn't bury our heads under bedclothes to keep warm". Paul steadily recovered, reverted to a conventional education and in 1914 went up – all too briefly – to St John's College, Cambridge. Profoundly grateful for the effectiveness of his treatment, his parents decided that other less-privileged children should share the benefits of an open-air life.

Basket-weaving class under an apple tree at Uffculme School.

Their solution was to offer to build an open-air school in the grounds of Uffculme, for the benefit of children whose living conditions in Birmingham had either weakened their health or were potentially damaging. In 1910 Barrow and Geraldine formally donated land for the new school to the Birmingham Education Committee, adding that "we are prepared to provide the simple buildings and furniture required for such a school, which we understand will cost about £400." The children were to arrive by train from central Birmingham, having been given cloth capes for the journey and with all their other clothing and equipment also to be provided by the Cadburys.

Instead of the usual Gothic or Revival style of architecture favoured for school buildings at that time, Barrow and Geraldine turned to a Birmingham firm of architects, Cossins, Peacock & Bewlay. Their designs were simple, functional and with a plan that linked a succession of pavilion-like classrooms. To give maximum air and light, the classrooms had sliding wood and glass screens on three sides, the intention being to have these open in all but the coldest weather and to give the children a degree of comfort by running hot-water pipes beneath the floor. This novel solution was attributed to Geraldine and was reckoned by some pupils to be less than successful.

When it first opened in September 1911, Uffculme Open-Air School took 28 children, most of them in poor health. The school records note their increasing weight and steady recovery from illnesses. Geraldine visited frequently, arranged for gardeners from Uffculme House to look after the grounds and encouraged the children to grow vegetables. At the end of an experimental year the open-air school was assessed and judged to be successful, both academically and in terms of benefiting the health of most of its pupils.

During the first 30 years of their marriage, Barrow and Geraldine Cadbury devoted increasingly large amounts of their income to educational institutions and to the care and treatment of young offenders. It was a pattern of giving that was to develop and grow throughout the rest of their lives.

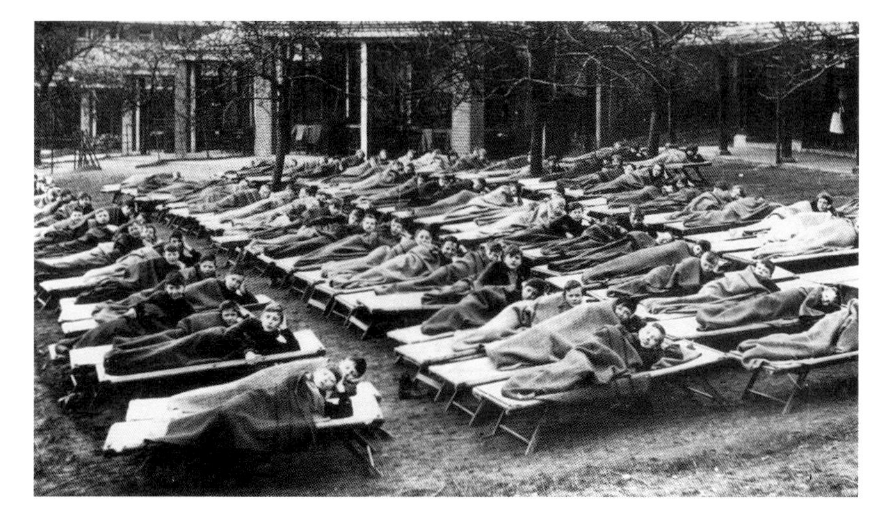

Rest time on stretchers in the open air at Uffculme School, March 1931.

Chapter 3
The Barrow & Geraldine S Cadbury Trust

In 1920 several factors combined to persuade Barrow and Geraldine that they should change the way they gave financial assistance to the people and projects they wished to support. They set up a charitable trust which they called the Barrow & Geraldine S Cadbury Trust. Shares in the British Cocoa and Chocolate Company, which were Barrow's personal holding, were transferred to the new trust to provide its capital. Because the profits of the company were ploughed back steadily into the business, the value of the shares – and so the endowment of the trust – began to increase steadily.

The timing of their decision was not a coincidence. As the First World War finally ground to some sort of conclusion, there was considerable debate among Quakers about how they should contribute to the new social order that was clearly emerging. In an article in the Quaker magazine *The Friend* in August 1918, Joseph Rowntree argued for a renewal of charitable giving, to complement what was expected from central and local government:

> *The more the State does for the individual the greater and not the less becomes his responsibility; an increase of privilege from the whole to the part creates an increase of debt from the part to the whole; the further communal enterprise develops, the more insistent is the need for voluntary spirit and for voluntary service.*

Woodbrooke in Selly Oak, Birmingham, bought by George Cadbury in 1881 as his family home and donated by him in 1903 as a college of training for Quaker ministry and as missionaries overseas.

Joseph Rowntree had set up his own charitable trust in 1904, three years after George Cadbury's Bournville Village Trust had been established. The two families not only drew on each other's ideas, but also shared initiatives. The Joseph Rowntree Charitable Trust had been a generous supporter of Woodbrooke, one of the Selly Oak colleges established by George Cadbury in 1903, in what had formerly been his family home in the suburbs of Birmingham and which became a centre for religious and social study. Barrow Cadbury was familiar with the work of the Rowntree Trust and the trust deed which set out its aims, the first of which was to provide support for an "institution known as the 'Woodbrooke Permanent Settlement'." The other objectives included:

> *... religious teaching; the improvement of ... schools; the foundation of scholarships; the study of the history of the Society of Friends; the promotion of temperance; peace and the settlement of international disputes; the investigation of the causes of poverty and distress ... and of the causes of irregularity of employment; the provision of public parks and pleasure grounds; the foundation of professorships, lectureships or scholarships; and the publication of ... reports, information, books, treatises, lectures, essays, or pamphlets.*

Virtually all these objectives, set out for the Joseph Rowntree Charitable Trust, were also to be adopted by the Barrow & Geraldine S Cadbury Trust.

Barrow and Geraldine were not the only members of the Cadbury family to respond to Joseph Rowntree's plea. Both the GW Cadbury Trust and the William Adlington Cadbury Trust were formed in the 1920s, when many wealthy Quaker families took steps to transform their charitable giving to meet the new political, social and economic circumstances. One of the reasons for this shift was that levels of taxation rose dramatically after the First World War, with Estate Duty increasing from 15 per cent to 40 per cent between 1914 and 1930. For Quaker families such as the Cadburys, a charitable trust was not simply a way of ensuring that the profits of their business were directed towards activities that were consistent with their beliefs, such as education, social improvement and temperance, rather than being spent by central government on armaments or an imperialist foreign policy. Barrow also made it consistently clear that he viewed the money he gave away via his charitable trusts as not his, but rather wealth which – through tax relief – had been entrusted to him for the benefit of society.

Barrow's personal fortune continued to grow throughout his time at Cadbury Bros Ltd. Having begun his career with menial tasks in every department of the business, by 1900 he had progressed to being one of four managing directors and the first secretary of the company. In 1918 he was made chairman of the Cadbury-Fry Joint Board, and in 1919 his daughter Dorothy and son Paul were appointed to the board of Cadbury Bros Ltd. On the death of his uncle George Cadbury in 1922, Barrow succeeded him as company chairman. At each stage of his business career, and with every advance, the transfer of capital to his and Geraldine's charitable trust increased correspondingly.

Although the Barrow & Geraldine S Cadbury Trust provided the couple with funds that enabled them to greatly extend their giving, it also constrained them. The principal restriction was that they could only support registered charities and not individuals. They wanted to be able to continue to give to those in need, very often people who had devoted their lives to the work of the Society of Friends and who, in old age, were without adequate pensions. In 1924 Barrow endowed a benevolent fund, which paid income tax at the full rate but was not assessed for surtax. After the legal status of such funds was challenged in the courts, Barrow transferred the assets to a benevolent company, named the Barrow Cadbury Fund Ltd, with a membership of 'directors' drawn from local Quakers. The fund enabled Barrow and Geraldine to continue the pattern of giving established in the early years of their marriage, but in a greatly expanded way.

In the early years of its operation the Barrow & Geraldine S Cadbury Trust was, to a considerable extent, reactive. Some of the donations made were to good causes that the family had supported for many years. These fell into four main categories. The first was concerned with hospitals, nursing and maternity care, and included:

Birmingham & District Augmentation Fund
Birmingham District Nursing Society
Birmingham Lying-in Charity and Maternity Hospital
Birmingham Medical Mission
Birmingham & Midland Hospital for Women
Bromsgrove Cottage Hospital
Birmingham Children's Hospital
Floodgate Street Maternity and Infant Welfare Centre
Highbury, Uffculme & Sorrento Hospital Comforts Fund
Queen's Hospital, Birmingham
The Retreat Mental Hospital, Yorkshire

The sums given were usually relatively small, ranging from £2.2.0 or £3.0.0 to £100.0.0, and changed little from year to year. In most cases a letter seeking help was sent to Barrow annually; he would then check his meticulous records for what he had contributed previously, and a cheque would be duly sent. The same process applied to the donations made to various Friends' funds, which included:

Friends' Emergency and War Victims Committee
Friends' Foreign Mission Association
Friends' Sunday School Union (Birmingham)
Friends' Temperance Union
Friends' Tract Association

Charitable giving of this sort, of donations rarely exceeding £200, was open to the criticism that it was not only reactive but relatively perfunctory, and little more than a continuation of the traditions of Victorian philanthropy. The list of donations became more personal and significant when the Barrow & Geraldine S Cadbury Trust began to commit much larger sums to penal reform and to education. In the former category were contributions to the Birmingham Discharged Prisoners' Aid Society, the Borstal Association and the Howard League for Penal Reform.

Guided by Geraldine, Barrow Cadbury increasingly saw improvements in the living conditions and education of deprived children as the key to preventing disease and crime. Members of the Cadbury family had served on the general committee of the Agatha Stacey Homes since their foundation in 1893. The aim of this charity was "to provide safe, and if needful, permanent shelters for those women and girls who through weak intellect have no power of self-protection." The donations from the Barrow & Geraldine S Cadbury Trust were modest, but continued until the 1950s. They also contributed, over a period of 30 years, to the Girls' Night Shelter in Tennant Street, Birmingham.

Numerous Quaker schools also benefited, including The Mount in York (Geraldine's *alma mater*, and where she made significant and life-lasting friendships) and Ackworth in West Yorkshire. Substantial sums were given to the five Selly Oak colleges on the outskirts of Birmingham: Carey Hall, Fircroft, Kingsmead, Westhill and Woodbrooke. Westhill, founded in 1907, was established for the training of Sunday School teachers and built on a site provided by George Cadbury; it was initially funded by Barrow and Geraldine.

Westhill College, Birmingham, established in 1907 by George Cadbury and George Hamilton Archibald to train Sunday School teachers. Barrow and Geraldine Cadbury made significant contributions to the college's work, both before and after they established their own charitable trust in 1920.

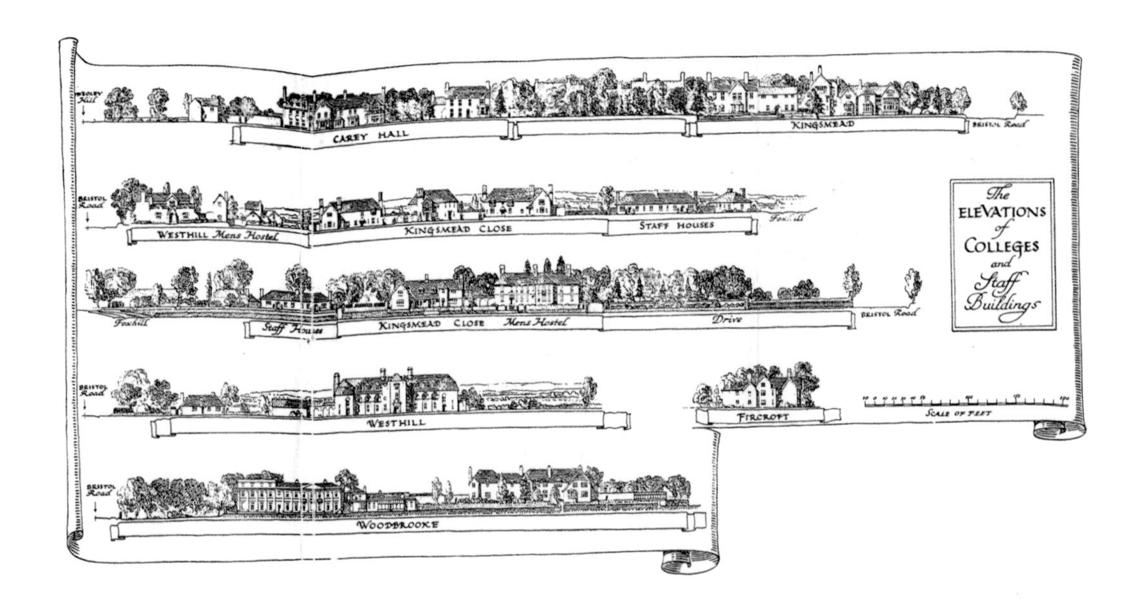

Elevational drawings of the colleges and staff buildings at Selly Oak, Birmingham, all of which were founded and funded by members of the Cadbury family: (top to bottom) *Carey Hall – a missionary training college for women, founded in 1912; Westhill College – founded in 1907 to train Sunday School teachers; Kingsmead – founded in 1905 for the training of Quaker missionaries going abroad; Fircroft – a residential adult education college founded in 1909; and Woodbrooke College – founded in 1903 as a place of training for Quaker ministry.*

One donation in these early years of the Trust stands out for being much larger than the rest. In 1922 the sum of £3,000 was provided for the building of a residential home for children at Cropwood, which had been Barrow and Geraldine's country home since 1907. The idea for the school had been Geraldine's and developed from her realisation that many of the health benefits to children attending the Uffculme Open-Air School were undone once they returned to the pollution of central Birmingham. Cropwood was to extend the provisions made at Uffculme, with similar classrooms, but with sleeping accommodation in long dormitories designed for up to eight children each.

At both Uffculme and Cropwood, Barrow and Geraldine showed how willing they were to use their funds in ways which were outside the remit of the Joseph Rowntree Charitable Trust. While they shared many of its educational aims, they had none of Rowntree's reluctance to spend money on architectural projects, as stipulated in his memorandum of 1904, in which he expressed his "regret if it were necessary to make grants on account of buildings." At Woodbrooke College he had resisted contributing to bricks and mortar, but was happy to fund scholarships and the purchase of books for the library. By contrast, Geraldine involved herself in every detail of the design of Cropwood, stipulating dark polished woodwork and tiles, rather than painted finishes that were easily marked and needed more maintenance. All the furniture was bought by her, and she personally selected the green serge dresses and figured crêpe frocks from Liberty; they were the sort of pretty clothes she would have chosen

Above *Children at Cropwood House Open-Air School in the 1920s, dressed for church in summer uniforms and straw hats.*

Left *Cropwood House Open-Air School in the 1950s, showing the loggia of open classrooms and dormitories.*

for her own children. She also provided the books for lessons, insisted on a fountain in the garden, and did everything she could to make Cropwood not just a healthy alternative to slum property in Birmingham, but a welcoming and homely one. This was how Barrow and Geraldine had thought of their family home at Cropwood, and was what they wanted to share. At the formal opening of the school on 17 June 1922, at which the buildings and 75 acres of grounds were handed over to the City of Birmingham's Education Committee, Barrow summed up their shared aims:

> *... that by God's blessing many generations of delicate city children may gain health of body and mind here. Cropwood will always be associated by us with memories of very happy days here.*

For their next major building project, Barrow and Geraldine used not their charitable trust, but the Barrow Cadbury Fund Ltd. This may have been because the building was not strictly a charitable institution, but a Children's Court for Birmingham. In 1922 Geraldine had been made a member of the Home Office Committee on Probation, becoming chairman of the Juvenile Court Panel of Justices in the following year, a post she held until 1936. As had become her practice, she insisted that the family circumstances of the children brought before the court were thoroughly investigated. She also kept in touch with children who had been sent to a reform school, farm training colony or other Home Office institution, and she kept the letters they wrote to her. On their release, she often helped them to find jobs and continued to send letters, postcards from abroad and birthday greetings. This may sound patronising and even sentimental, but Geraldine's approach was in fact increasingly professional. She employed two full-time secretaries to assist in her court work and the investigations that accompanied it, and built up and used a considerable library of books on child delinquency and children's law as applied in Britain and other countries around the world. When Barrow went on business to Australia and the United States, she travelled with him and arranged to see for herself examples of enlightened provision for juvenile offenders, wherever they were to be found.

As was now usual, Geraldine personally supervised every detail of the design of the Children's Court. There were to be waiting-rooms for children and their parents, committee rooms which could also be used for out-of-court discussions, and rooms reserved for the use of probation officers. A hostel for girls was provided on the top floors, where they could be held on remand. The court-room itself was top-lit, with a simple dais for the table used by the magistrates and no dock, witness box or jury box. It was impressive without being overpowering. In July 1928 the Home

Secretary Sir William Joynson-Hicks opened the new court at 58 Newton Street, Birmingham – it was the first purpose-built Children's Court in the country, and had been entirely paid for by the Barrow Cadbury Fund.

Between 1922 and her death in 1941, Geraldine found herself increasingly called on by the Home Office to join its boards and committees. These included the Departmental Committee on the Treatment of Young Offenders, on which she served for eight years; the Advisory Committee on Probation (from 1922 to 1941); and the Probation Training Board (from 1930 to 1941). She also joined a committee convened by the Home Office in 1928 to enquire into the working of police courts and juvenile courts in the Metropolitan Police District. In 1932 she served on the Juvenile Court Rules Committee, and in 1934 she contributed to the Home Office conference on girls aged 15 to 17 appearing before London's juvenile courts. By that time, Geraldine's experience and wisdom was recognised internationally, and in 1935 she was elected vice-president of the International Association of Children's Courts Judges.

The first purpose-built Children's Court, at 58 Newton Court, Birmingham, paid for entirely by the Barrow Cadbury Fund and opened by the Home Secretary in 1928.

With this growing recognition came a dilemma. There was a long-standing and deep-rooted antipathy among many Quakers to the use of titles. Their resistance to any of the badges of status had extended in the past to accepting prison sentences rather than raise a hat or show any other marks of respect. Consequently the offer to Geraldine in May 1937 of the honour of Dame Commander of the Order of the British Empire (DBE) was problematic, not least because she felt that her achievements had been part of the ideals she shared with Barrow, and much of what she had done would not have been possible without his money. He must have encouraged her to accept it, however, and the honour was duly conferred the following May. Shortly afterwards, when she made one of her regular visits to the women's class at the Moseley Road Friends' Institute, the apprehensive class secretary asked how she would like to be addressed. Geraldine's answer was characteristic: "I'm Mrs Barrow Cadbury as usual. We'll have no Dame School here!"

Towards the end of Geraldine's life, the value of the assets held by the Barrow & Geraldine S Cadbury Trust increased rapidly year by year. In 1921 they had been valued at £23,124. Ten years later their value stood at £52,604, and on her death in 1941 they had reached £168,845 and were producing an annual income of £24,007, from which donations amounting to £13,874 were disbursed. At that time the trustees were Barrow and Geraldine and their three children, Dorothy, Paul and Cherry. Donations were made to over 230 charities, ranging in size from subscriptions of a few pounds to various temperance organisations, to rather larger contributions to anti-slavery societies and missions for seamen, and many thousands of pounds to the Birmingham Maternity Hospital. In 1938 further grants of £10,000 from the Barrow Cadbury Fund went to both the Birmingham Hospitals Centre and the Birmingham Maternity Hospital building fund.

In 1940 over 80 individuals received donations from the Barrow Cadbury Fund, in most cases explained in the company's minutes by the somewhat cryptic note, "moral obligation". In a few instances there was a further brief explanation: Mrs EC Mildren, "widow of splendid and unselfish Birmingham temperance worker", received £30. Several recipients had worked, no doubt for very modest salaries, for various adult schools. Mrs Goodchild, who had been Barrow's secretary at Bournville for many years, was given £10. An old schoolfriend of Geraldine's, Miss Ethel Harding, was sent £50; and a cousin, Miss Theodora Graham, received £200. Miss Elizabeth Kershaw, a probation officer whom Geraldine particularly valued, was given £37.14.0. The payments appear to have been a mixture of one-off donations and annuities, underlining the point that the Fund provided long-term financial support for some of its beneficiaries.

(Reginald) Clifford Allen, 1st Baron Allen of Hurtwood (1889–1939), a Quaker politician and peace campaigner, thrice imprisoned as a conscientious objector, and supported in later life with an annuity from the Barrow Cadbury Fund.

Barrow greatly admired Clifford Allen (1889–1939), a Quaker politician and peace campaigner, who took a completely uncompromising position against war with Germany. During the First World War, Allen had chaired the No-Conscription Fellowship, which condemned militarism in all its forms. In 1916 he had been arrested, court-martialled and sentenced to two years' hard labour, during which he contracted a disease of the lungs. His health never recovered, although he continued to publish books and essays on international politics. He was raised to the peerage as Baron Allen of Hurtwood in 1932 and in his last speech in the House of Lords, in July 1938, he condemned Nazi antisemitism. Barrow Cadbury sent him £150 from his fund in 1937 and a further £200 the following year. After Allen's death in 1939, his widow was given £150.

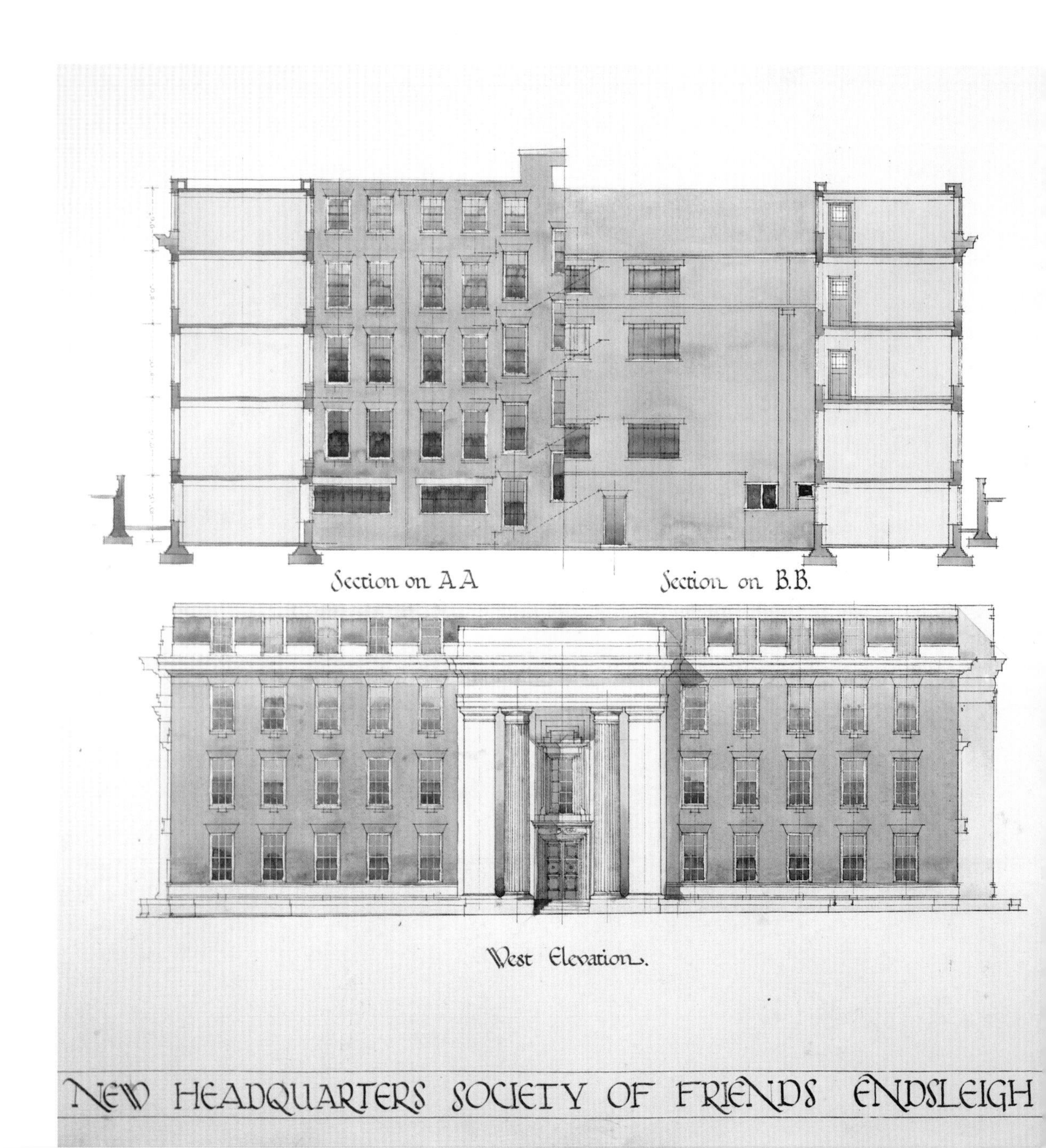

Elevations and sections for the new headquarters of The Society of Friends in Euston Road, London, designed by Hubert Lidbetter in 1923 and opened in 1926.

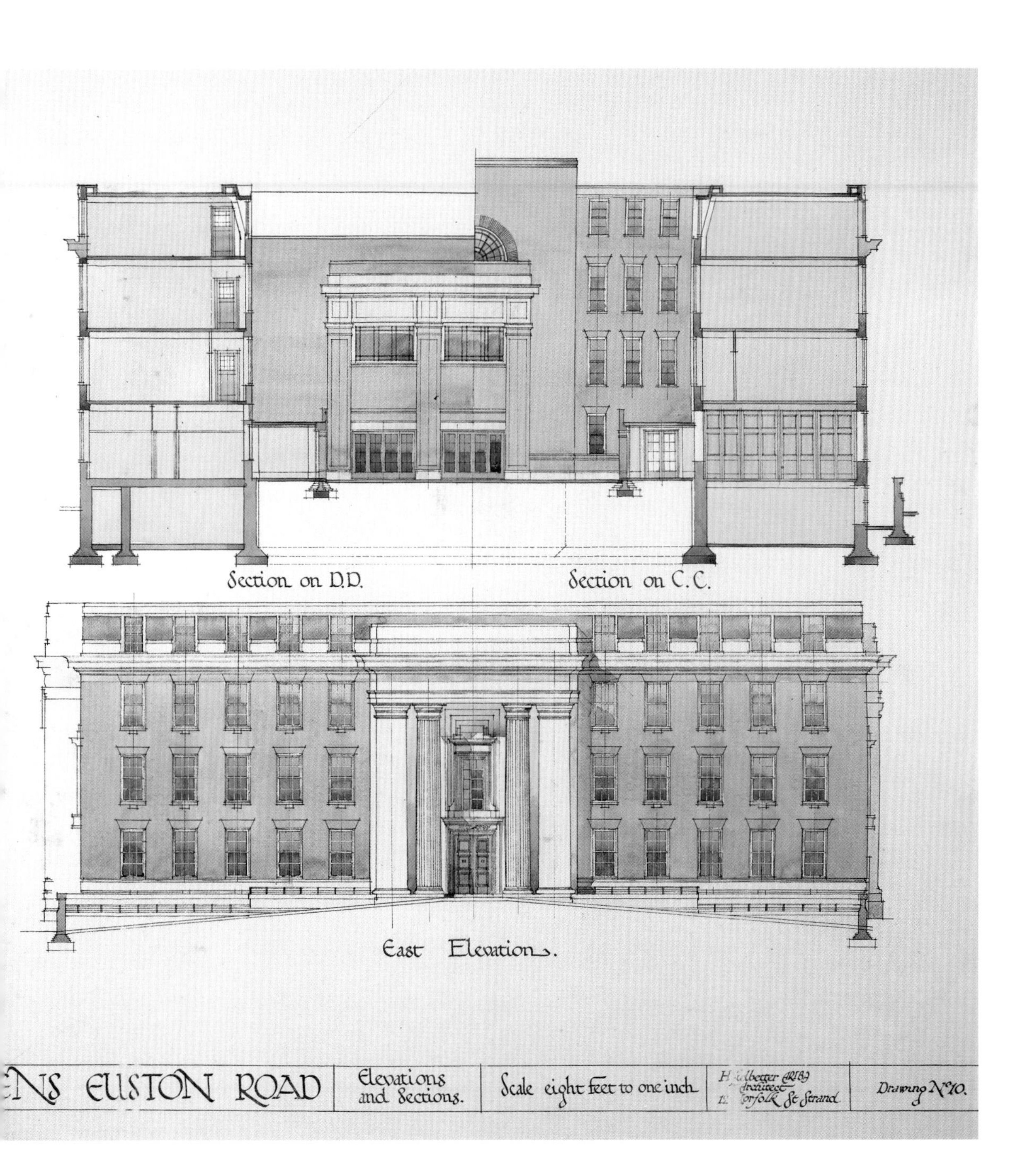
Section on D.D.
Section on C.C.
East Elevation.
NS EUSTON ROAD
Elevations and Sections.
Scale eight feet to one inch
St Strand
Drawing No 10.

Some of those who benefited from the Barrow Cadbury Fund had served the Society of Friends all their lives, yet received little or no pension and were experiencing real hardship. This perhaps explains the "moral obligation" felt by Barrow and Geraldine. The Fund contributed to the staff pensions of those employed by the Society, and in 1924 Barrow became treasurer of the appeal committee for the construction of the new Friends' House on Euston Road in London. By 1926 – when it was opened – £60,848 had been raised. Barrow chose to contribute from his own resources, without recourse to either his charitable trust or his fund.

After Barrow Cadbury retired from the chairmanship of Cadbury Bros Ltd in 1932, his charitable giving became even more central to his life. That year he received the Freedom of the City of Birmingham, in recognition of what he had contributed, both as a businessman and a philanthropist. However, both he and Geraldine were wary of being described in that way, because of the associations with Victorian philanthropy. As their son Paul wrote in 1970:

> *Because my parents, and particularly my mother, were among the first social reformers to react against anything that was connected with patronage, they disliked being described as philanthropists.*

What made a deep impression on Barrow and Geraldine's children and grandchildren was their commitment to doing far more than distributing alms or other forms of charity to the poor. Paul remembered as a child of 11 being driven along Moseley Street in Birmingham with his mother, who talked to him of the impossibility of achieving social justice for people living in back-to-back houses in the slum districts of the city. To her mind, any solution to the problems of the poor of Birmingham depended on action by central and local government to improve housing, education and health care. That was why Geraldine was prepared to wear herself out serving on Home Office committees.

Barrow and Geraldine also believed that giving meant much more than distributing grants from their charitable trust. Again, their son Paul thought it was important to record his mother's highly personal response to social breakdown:

> *Her instinct was always positive and she did not believe that the puritanism of Victorian reformers was achieving results. If they swept the crumbs under the carpet where they could not be seen, she had a way of turning up the carpet. Her children knew, as adolescents, that she had friends who were prostitutes, and she was the friend and supporter of the unmarried mother and her illegitimate child, rather than their critic. Rehabilitation rather than censure was what mattered.*

The combination of work on committees, which involved travelling backwards and forwards to London, and the attention Geraldine gave to the welfare of those she encountered through the courts – before, during and after the exercise of her official duties as a magistrate – took their toll. The burden became still greater with the outbreak of the Second World War, when many of the probation officers and other staff left their jobs because of conscription. Even the Blitz did not stop Geraldine going to London in an attempt to ensure that the work of penal reform was not set aside. At her instigation the Birmingham Maternity Hospital, which she and Barrow had supported with large donations since it opened in 1907, was moved from the centre of the city, where there was intense bombing, to a house called Long Mede, some 12 miles away. The costs of these provisions were met with a grant of £10,995 from the Barrow & Geraldine S Cadbury Trust and a further £10,000 from the Barrow Cadbury Fund.

The last time Geraldine left the house in Edgbaston Park Road that she and Barrow had bought in 1929 to be close to Paul and his family, was to see 20 mothers and babies safely transferred to Long Mede. Illness – almost certainly brought on by overwork – confined her to bed, but did not stop her discussing plans with Barrow for an observation centre for problem children on remand. On 21 January 1941 she had a stroke and died at home nine days later.

Barrow outlived Geraldine for a further 17 years. The observation centre at Forhill House, near King's Norton in Birmingham, which he presented to the city, was in memory of his wife. It was, he said at the opening ceremony on 30 May 1947, to "fulfil a desire that was dear to my wife's heart." In 1946 the Barrow & Geraldine S Cadbury Trust donated £9,000 to the centre, and a further £14,000 the following year. Further contributions were made annually thereafter.

Speaking at the opening of Forhill House, the Home Secretary James Chuter Ede announced that the government was to fund further observation centres, as had been recommended by the committees on which Geraldine had served. He concluded:

> *Geraldine Cadbury did probably more for delinquent children than anybody in this country or in any other. She was ahead of her time, but her faith will be justified.*

Chapter 4
Passing the Baton

Barrow Cadbury (second left) *on his 90th birthday, with his children, Paul, Dorothy and Cherry.*

Neither Barrow nor Geraldine pushed their children into involvement with their charitable work, but relationships within the family were such that the younger generations were drawn in gradually and willingly. Half a century after Barrow and Geraldine's deaths, their grandchildren spoke of both of them with deep affection and respect, bordering on awe. "She was charming" and "absolutely lovely", recalled Catherine Hickinbotham and Philippa Southall of their grandmother. Barrow meanwhile was remembered as being "loving, caring and possibly over-protective."

Dorothy, Paul and Cherry were appointed trustees of the Barrow & Geraldine S Cadbury Trust by a deed dated 22 December 1934, which names Barrow as chairman and treasurer, and Paul as secretary. The three children attended their first meeting on 17 March 1935. To mark the appointment of new trustees, Barrow transferred a further 10,000 Ordinary (fully paid-up) £1 shares in British Cocoa and Chocolate Co Ltd to the Trust. It was agreed that the trustees should meet at least once a year, and that if necessary the decision of the majority would be binding. Major decisions had to be approved by Barrow and Geraldine, and the children were certainly not expected to sign cheques. At this time Dorothy was 42, Paul 39 and Cherry 34.

In 1943, two years after Geraldine's death, Barrow transferred another 21,220 Ordinary £1 shares to the Trust, in the knowledge that if he died within a year they would be liable to Estate Duty. Conscious that there was a vacancy, Paul's wife Rachel was invited by Barrow to join the trustees, as was confirmed in a deed dated 19 December 1944. A year later the assets of the Barrow & Geraldine S Cadbury Trust amounted to £204,217 and donations to £15,011. The first paid member of staff was Joyce R Taylor, previously Barrow's secretary, who in 1951 began to provide part-time clerical help.

As well as taking these rather formal steps to engage the next generation, younger members of the family were encouraged to learn what was involved in the work of the Trust. When Philippa Southall, the third of Paul and Rachel Cadbury's children, was barely in her teens, she was invited into her grandmother's office, where there was a "nice secretary called Miss Brusa." The experience made an indelible impression on Philippa, which she vividly recollected when in her 80s. "Go in and look at the card-index and you'll see what we do," Geraldine told her. Philippa recalled that "it was my first experience of how a card-index worked; when I opened [it], she had card-indexed *every* child that she saw at the Juvenile Court and their parents and their friends."

A further reason for Paul and Dorothy's close involvement in the Trust and the Fund was that both were immersed in working for the firm of Cadbury, and what it stood for financially and socially. Dorothy began work at Bournville in January 1917, moving between the confectionery, cocoa, vegetable-drying and tin-soldering departments, before becoming a managing director of Cadbury Bros Ltd in 1919. Paul joined the family firm the same year, having spent most of the First World War in the Friends' Ambulance Unit. By 1921 he had progressed to the joint board of Cadbury and Fry and had revolutionised the sales department, equipping it to take advantage of the new export markets that were to open up between the two World Wars. Like his father, Paul's work for the company brought him considerable personal wealth, which he began to direct, relatively early in his career, towards the charitable causes that were important to him.

The youngest of Paul and Rachel's six children, Margaret, was born in 1930, a year after their fifth child, Roger, had died a few days after his birth. When Margaret was diagnosed as having cerebral palsy, Paul reacted in very much the way that his mother would have done. He involved himself in the care of other similarly affected children, becoming a prime mover in their education and welfare. He was the first chairman of the Midland

Spastic Association, was its long-serving president and during 1952–53 served on the Ministry of Health Committee on the welfare needs of those with cerebral palsy.

Another of Paul's personal interests was the care of the blind, to which he gave generously, particularly between 1920 and 1940. Within the Birmingham Institution he chaired the Trade Committee and served as a member of the Education Committee. Some of these concerns had not been supported by the Barrow & Geraldine S Cadbury Trust or the Barrow Cadbury Fund and, rather than trying to redirect their giving, Paul preferred to set up his own trust. In 1931, and probably prompted by the birth of Margaret the previous year, Paul established a charity in his own name, the Paul S Cadbury Trust. Like his father, he transferred shares to it over many years and its resources grew substantially. The Midland Spastic Association was a major beneficiary, as were the Middlemore Emigration Homes, although these were also supported by the Barrow & Geraldine S Cadbury Trust with substantial donations in the 1930s and 1940s.

Sir John Middlemore, founder of the first 'Children's Emigration Home' in Birmingham in 1872, photographed with boys he sent to Canada in the 1870s.

The Middlemore Emigration Homes, and the very idea of taking children from their families, transporting them to the other side of the world and either institutionalising them or (occasionally) placing them with what proved to be abusive adoptive parents, has rightly been the subject of fierce criticism. The terrible damage done to some of those taken to Australia and Canada is now well known, and public apologies have been made by the Australian Prime Minister. However, what is indisputable is the entirely well-intentioned aims of those responsible for the Middlemore Emigration Homes in St Luke's Road, Birmingham. The homes had been established in 1872 to save boys and girls from the often appalling living conditions in the city's slums. As the 1925 annual report for the homes explained, they were to "emigrate children from a Birmingham slum to a Canadian farmhouse. Furthermore, the home is selected after careful enquiries."

It is not difficult to see why the scheme attracted the support of the Barrow & Geraldine S Cadbury Trust. The whole concept of Bournville Village, and of Uffculme and Cropwood Open-Air Schools, was that children should be taken from a wretched environment to a healthy one, where there was employment and the promise of a better life.

Middlemore House in Selly Oak, Birmingham, originally built as an 'Emigration Home' and subsequently used as a short-stay residential home for schoolchildren. After 1954 the building was used as the library of Westhill College, but was demolished in 2004.

The report of 1925 went on to say that:

> *Our children are drawn from a large area around Birmingham, as well as from the city, and come chiefly through the agency of the National Society for the Prevention of Cruelty to Children, the Children's Courts, probation officers, Police Court Missioners, and Boards of Guardians.*

Some of the cases described show how hopeless the families of the children were, with instances of violent abuse and extreme neglect. The Homes in Birmingham, to which the children were initially taken, were in extensive grounds and carefully furnished and equipped. As vice-chairman of the Committee of Management, Paul Cadbury gave annual donations from the Barrow & Geraldine S Cadbury Trust amounting to many thousands of pounds, and used business trips to Canada to discuss the scheme with the Minister for Immigration and to inspect homes where there were children from Birmingham. The chairman of the House Committee was Paul's wife Rachel. If the reports were unduly optimistic and only hint at the ways in which the scheme failed some children, there were unquestionably others who benefited from the Middlemore Homes. The policies changed during the 50 years that Paul and Rachel served on their committees, with a gradual realisation that most children – although not all – were best looked after within their own families.

Another of Paul's initiatives was the setting up of a trust to hold and manage Walton Farm in the Clent Hills of Worcestershire, an area threatened by the accelerating spread of suburban Birmingham. Paul's response was to buy the farm in 1938, operate it through the specially constituted Worgan

Trust (the constitution of the Barrow & Geraldine S Cadbury Trust did not allow for the ownership of land) and to agree protective covenants – requiring consent to any proposed development – with the National Trust. As Paul Cadbury noted many years later, in 1970:

> *The present interests of the present Trustees and the Directors of the Fund ... represent in many cases a development of the concerns of the founders. Their children and their grandchildren grew up knowing that these concerns and their own interests have developed on similar, if not identical, lines.*

Part of that process of evolution and transformation derived from gradually changing Quaker attitudes. The lives of Barrow and Geraldine's children were shaped by the ideals of the Society of Friends, and these continued to provide the guiding principles of the Trust and the Fund. Paul and Rachel remained committed, practicing Quakers all their lives. Their marriage on 24 June 1919, at the George Road Meeting House in Birmingham, was described shortly afterwards by Paul's great-uncle George Cadbury:

> *The meeting was one of the best types of Quaker Meeting, because during the long periods of silence in the half hour, there was apparently a spirit of worship over the gathering, one might almost have heard a pin drop, and the addresses were all very short. The bride and bridegroom spoke up well. They are a delightful couple, with great opportunities of usefulness before them, at a time when the help of good people is needed all the world over.*

Paul and Rachel Cadbury on their wedding day, 24 June 1919, at George Road Meeting House, Birmingham.

Paul Cadbury on holiday with four of his children in 1928: (left to right) *Catherine, Charles, Edward and Philippa*

Two of their children, Catherine and Philippa, attended the Meeting at Moseley Road on Sunday mornings with their parents, spending part of the time in the children's class run by their mother. Catherine recalled that "I had to sit very quiet on a hassock. I was occasionally allowed a peppermint or something. But it was pain and grief ... we did have a piano and we did sing hymns, very badly." Those children who were unmusical were encouraged to make a contribution by announcing a hymn, and the most memorable part of the Meeting was the prayers that Barrow had prepared in advance. They made a great impression on his granddaughter Philippa: "Grandpa was absolutely reliable on praying ... his prayers were wonderful." Barrow could also intervene decisively, as he did at the World Conference of Friends held in Oxford in 1952. There had been disagreements that seemed to be leading to an impasse, but at that moment Barrow's voice was heard from the heart of the gathering: "O God, we are in a fix; please help us to find a way out of it." There was complete silence for ten minutes. It was enough to resolve the dispute.

Paul, however, took a more relaxed view of some Quaker practices than his father, partly because he was aware of how easy it was to be inconsistent. Barrow believed that there should be no work on Sundays and refrained from using his car that day so his chauffeur did not have to drive him. He instead used his bicycle for any journey, having never learnt to drive himself. But he did expect there to be a full family lunch – always of roast beef and chicken – at his home Southfield, which was prepared by his household staff. He also disapproved of buying a Sunday newspaper, in spite of Paul's gentle observation, "But it's printed on Saturday; it's the Monday paper you shouldn't buy, Father." When the family left the Sunday Meeting in Moseley Road to go home, Paul quietly told his children, "Just let Grandpa get ahead, and then I can go and buy my paper." A similar game was played whenever the fire engine was called out on Sunday morning. The fire station was next to the Moseley Road Meeting House and if there was an emergency when they were walking back home, Paul would say: "Wait till Grandpa's out of the way, and we'll go and have a look." No doubt Barrow was not deceived for a moment, but simply knew that he and Paul felt differently about such things.

What did not change significantly was the conduct of the meetings of the various trusts. They usually took place on Sunday afternoons. "If you weren't prompt, you weren't popular," Philippa recalled of her first meetings in the 1960s, going on to explain that:

> *They would be conducted like any Quaker business meeting. The minutes were gone through and everything was discussed, and then you had cold supper, produced by my father. Actually he had someone produce it the day before.*

As he had done for his father since 1935, Paul would take the minutes. The following morning they would be typed up by Carole Yates, his secretary. Although Cadbury as a business retained a very collaborative style of management, with a large Works Council that dealt with everything from

View from the Clent Hills, where Paul Cadbury bought land in 1938 in an area threatened by the spread of suburban Birmingham, seen in the distance.

discipline to bonuses, the running of the family's charitable trusts was confined to an intimate inner circle.

The Cadbury family were clearly in earnest about their charitable giving, but they also took their sporting activities seriously. Barrow was an enthusiastic skater and cyclist, Paul was an accomplished cricketer, and his wife Rachel was a fine horsewoman who was still – much to the consternation of her children – riding side-saddle in her 80s. It is little surprise therefore that playing fields were provided early in the development of Bournville. When Paul eventually retired from the chairmanship of Cadbury in 1965, at the age of 70, he was succeeded by his cousin Adrian, George Cadbury's grandson, whose accomplishments as an Olympic oarsman were a source of pride to the family.

Chapter 5
War, Peace and International Understanding

In its early years, the Barrow & Geraldine S Cadbury Trust contributed regularly to organisations concerned with international relations and the pursuit of peace. These included the British Institute of International Affairs, the International Arbitration League, the League of Nations Union, the National Peace Council and the Peace Society. Barrow's commitment to peace initiatives was strengthened by his understanding and knowledge of Germany and its language – he and Geraldine visited the country frequently, organised exchange visits to Bournville and admired the German sense of civic order and the importance attached to good schools. That there should have been two calamitous wars with Germany during their lifetimes was a matter of profound distress to both of them.

Since the seventeenth century pacifism had been central to Quaker beliefs, but in the late nineteenth century these principles took on renewed relevance. The Cadbury family, and in particular George and his wife Elizabeth, were appalled by the press clamour for war against the Boers in 1899. Encouraged by the Liberal politician David Lloyd George, Cadbury was eventually prevailed upon to buy the *Daily News*, principally to give accurate accounts of the financial interests of those supporting the war in South Africa and the way in which it was being conducted. "This was seen as the most diabolical war ever waged," George Cadbury wrote, and the exposure of the cruelty of British concentration camps – in which an estimated 26,000 Afrikaners and 13,000 Africans died – justified his view. Public realisation that the Boer War of 1899–1902, and the accompanying deaths of 22,000 British soldiers, was not the easy triumph that had been predicted, meant that at the beginning of the twentieth century pacifism had become more acceptable morally and socially.

As the threat of war with Germany grew increasingly real, Barrow found himself invited to join peace conferences because of his fluent German. He attended the Seventeenth Universal Congress for Peace in London in 1908 and was one of those invited to a reception at Buckingham Palace.

The following year he joined a party of representatives from the British Committee of Churches on a visit to Berlin, and in a letter home to Geraldine he wrote of the welcome given by the Kaiser and his speech advocating greater understanding between nations. The outbreak of the First World War in August 1914 found Barrow and Geraldine in Holland – just two months earlier, they had been in Berlin and Hamburg with an Adult School party.

The war brought fundamental disagreements within the Society of Friends over what the right response to German aggression should be. There were also divisions within Quaker families, and even differences of view between Barrow and Geraldine. Many Quakers retained an uncompromising rejection of war and militarism in all its forms, and in due course often became supporters of the No-Conscription Fellowship. For them anything that could be interpreted as tacit support for war was a betrayal of a central tenet of Quaker belief. A less extreme view was represented by the Friends' War Victims Relief Committee, which had been set up to help those suffering from the Balkan conflict that preceded the outbreak of war with Germany in 1914. Many Quakers rejected military service, but found that they could reconcile their conflicting loyalties by joining the Friends' Ambulance Unit (FAU), organised and led by Philip Noel-Baker and financially supported by both George Cadbury and Arnold Rowntree.

A Friends' Ambulance Unit vehicle, with the organisation's symbol painted on the door, deployed during the First World War.

Jordans Training Camp in Buckinghamshire, where members of the Society of Friends were trained for six weeks in first aid, sanitation, hygiene and field cookery, before being deployed to Belgium in October 1914 as the 'First Anglo-Belgian Ambulance Unit'. Paul Cadbury is the central figure in the back row.

War broke out just as Paul Cadbury arrived at St John's College, Cambridge. He left after one day to join the Friends' War Victims Relief Committee in France, a decision approved of by his father but with Paul later hinting that his mother reacted differently to the moral dilemmas with which they were wrestling:

> *During the Great War, BC identified himself with Quaker relief work. GSC was more inclined to support PSC when he ceased working with the Friends' War Victims Relief Committee and joined the Friends' Ambulance Unit in 1915, and in 1916 she started the FAU Uffculme Hospital for wounded soldiers.*

The offer of the former Uffculme Open-Air School, which had been closed since December 1914 and subsequently used as a distributing centre for Belgian refugees, included alterations and re-equipment, carried out and paid for by Barrow and Geraldine. It was ready to receive the first convoy of wounded men by December 1916 and the following year the tea-rooms in the grounds were converted into additional wards. By using marquees on the front lawns, the number of beds was increased to 200. Immediately after the war Uffculme was adapted into an orthopaedic-treatment and prosthetic limb-fitting centre serving six Midland counties.

1/1/300

NAME. Cadbury. Paul Strangman

ADDRESS. 64 Wheeleys Road Birmingham.

NEW ADDRESS.

Brassard No. 7122. Date 191

Cap Badge No. 324. Unit No. ~~358~~ 434

Identity Disc No. 7122 Passport No. ~~462~~ 152676

Exemption Absolute Grounds Consc. Obj. Certificate No. 45 War Office

Date of Birth Nov. 3rd 1895 Nationality British Married or Single Single.

Nearest relative father Address: G. Cadbury 64 Wheeleys Road Birmingham.

Vaccination Infancy + 1914

1st. Inoculation Oct. 1914

2nd. Inoculation " "

Re-Inoculation Nov. 1915 Nov. 1916 20.3.18

Kit Expenses to Self. ~~G. Cadbury~~

Period of Service Contract from 1.XI.15.

Religion Member Society of Friends Attender

Previous occupation F.W.V.R.C. Undergraduate

QUALIFICATIONS.

Hospital 1st Aid cert.

Motors Instr. School Exam. 81.%

Languages French Flemish.

Special Rough carpentry.

Training Jordans 1.XI.15. to 27.XI.15.

Uniform supplied

B.R.C.S. 20.XI. 1915

B.R.C.S. 1.VIII. 1917.

191

191

191

191

1/1/296

NAME. Cadbury. Laurence John.

ADDRESS. Northfield Manor Birmingham.

NEW ADDRESS.

Brassard No. 1134. Date 191

Cap Badge No. 642. Unit No. ~~193~~. 44

Identity Disc No. 1649. Passport No. 168190 ~~9874~~. 26.III.15. 26.IX.17.

Exemption Absolute Grounds Indispensable Certificate No. 277 War Office

Date of Birth March 30th 1889 Nationality British Married or Single Single

Nearest relative Address: Northfield Manor Birmingham.

Vaccination 20 Mar 18 1903.

1st. Inoculation Oct. 1914.

2nd. Inoculation " "

Re-Inoculation 23 Mar 18 Oct. 1916

Kit Expenses to: Self

Period of Service Contract from 7.IX.14.

Religion Member Society of Friends Attender

Previous occupation Manufacturer

QUALIFICATIONS.

Hospital B.R.C.S. cert.

Motors

Languages French - a little

Special

Training Jordans. IX.14. to X.14.

Uniform supplied

191

191

191

191

191

191

Top *Paul Cadbury's Friends' Ambulance Unit service card, and* **above** *Laurence Cadbury's Friends' Ambulance Unit service card.*

Paul Cadbury in the uniform of the Friends' Ambulance Unit, c.1914.

Paul Cadbury was based in Dunkirk, where his cousin Laurence was also deployed. Initially, he worked on an ambulance train, and in due course was summoned to the Western Front to drive an ambulance evacuating wounded soldiers from field dressing stations. He was 19 when he joined the FAU and never spoke of his experiences subsequently, except to acknowledge that he met his future wife Rachel Wilson while she was working as a nurse for the Unit at Dunkirk. The two Quaker families were, needless to say, already related by marriage. Rachel was described by George Cadbury as "a bright, healthy, vigorous, Christian girl, with plenty of pluck and with courage to hold her own opinions; a thorough going Friend."

As the full horror of the war unfolded, George Cadbury's objections to military service weakened. Bertie, his youngest son, initially joined the Royal Navy, then transferred to the Royal Naval Air Service, subsequently becoming – in the rank of captain – one of the first pilots of the Royal Air Force. He was awarded the Distinguished Flying Cross for shooting down one of the best-equipped Zeppelins in the German fleet. The Cadbury family showed in this, as with other concerns, a pragmatic response to moral choices which became increasingly complex as the war progressed.

Paul Cadbury and Rachel Wilson in France during the First World War, where they met whilst serving in the Friends' Ambulance Unit. Rachel joined the Unit as a nurse on 8 January 1917, and was later based at the Queen Alexandra Hospital in Malo-les-Bains.

With the end of hostilities in 1918, Barrow resumed his support for peace initiatives, an act that inevitably led him to association with appeasement. He was attracted to the policy advocated by the politician and lifelong Christian pacifist George Lansbury – who had resigned his leadership of the Labour Party in 1935 because of disagreements over pacifism – and who proposed, "You will have to meet around a table after the war; why not meet now when you can save the peace?" What Barrow Cadbury and others could not comprehend was that Hitler and Mussolini had no intention of preserving peace. In the late 1930s the Barrow Cadbury Fund made annual donations of £750 to Lansbury's Embassies of Reconciliation, delegations led by Lansbury to many heads of governments in Europe in an attempt to persuade them to avert war. Barrow also attended the conferences held by the World Council of Churches, at which Bishop George Bell spoke. Like Bell, he knew at first hand that there were many Germans who loathed everything that the Nazis stood for and who were looking to other countries to give them moral and practical support.

Barrow Cadbury never wavered in his fundamental convictions: "In the first place my objective is the *total abolition* of war," he maintained. He had been deceived by the Kaiser in 1914, when he told the Birmingham newspapers: "The German Emperor is one of the greatest powers for peace at the present day, and absolutely sincere." He had the wool pulled over his eyes again by Hitler and the Nazis.

The impact of the Second World War on the Cadbury works at Bournville was such that the chocolate-moulding department was converted to manufacture gun doors for Spitfires, the chocolate-packing department was used for making gas masks, and camouflage netting was draped over the factory. Sheep grazed on the village green and the sports fields became vegetable plots.

A Friends' Ambulance Unit vehicle in action in France during the First World War.

However grim the outlook in 1939, the choices faced by the Society of Friends had become clearer, and therefore easier, than they had been in the First World War. The Friends' Ambulance Unit had showed that Quakers and other pacifists were prepared to face dangers and privations comparable to those experienced by the armed forces. The State had learnt that sending conscientious objectors to prison did nothing for the war effort and that understanding and leniency produced an organisation that could do much to relieve the suffering brought by war. The Military Training Act of May 1939 instigated tribunals and an appeals procedure for conscientious objectors. In July that year several Quakers involved in the old FAU wrote to the Ministry of Labour asking if "it is possible that there may be room for a voluntary scheme or schemes." However, they did so on the basis of their individual conscience and without the official sanction of the Yearly Meeting of the Society of Friends, which remained divided on what service might be appropriate for their members in a time of war.

For the Cadburys and the Rowntrees, used to making life-shaping decisions, the revival of the FAU was clearly justified. In August 1939 Paul Cadbury and Arnold Rowntree (1872–1951) met while on holiday in Anglesey. The two families discussed joint action, Paul's daughter Catherine later recalling how Arnold, an impressive man in every sense, turned to her father and said: "Oh Paul, you must start up the FAU again. It's desperate, we're going to have a lot of conscientious objectors and we've got to have something ready for them."

Paul Cadbury and Arnold Rowntree on holiday in Anglesey in August 1939, discussing the revival of the Friends' Ambulance Unit prior to the Second World War. This photograph was taken by Paul's daughter, Philippa.

In September a long letter, signed by Paul Cadbury and John Harvey, appeared in *The Friend* saying that no action was expected by the Society's Executive Committee, but that a group of individuals acting on their own initiative would be approaching the Ministry of Labour to request approval for the revival of the FAU. It ended with the suggestion that "if war comes, such a scheme would be rapidly developed to train men for relief and ambulance work." Yet the letter was overtaken by events before it was even published, when Britain and France declared war on Germany on 3 September 1939.

A member of the Friends' Ambulance Unit helping refugee children during the Second World War.

George Cadbury's widow, Dame Elizabeth Cadbury, immediately agreed to make available some unoccupied buildings at Manor Farm at Northfield in Birmingham, and financial help was pledged by the Bournville Village Trust. As the historian of the FAU, A Tegla Davies, recorded:

> *The mainspring was Paul Cadbury – here, there and everywhere – interviewing prospective members, attending tribunals, seeing officials, turning up at all hours of the day and night with new pieces of equipment for the camp.*

Paul was appointed chairman of the FAU council, with Arnold Rowntree, the elder statesman who had urged him on, as vice-chairman. In the first few days over 300 applicants joined. The Council would not accept men under direction from the Ministry of Labour's tribunals, and of 65,000 registered conscientious objectors, 1,300 were ultimately to serve in the FAU. The Barrow Cadbury Fund contributed £600 to the FAU in 1939 and £4,200 in 1940. The first donation from the Barrow & Geraldine S Cadbury Trust was in 1941, amounting to £2,000; in 1942 it was again

£2,000, the next year £2,300, followed by £1,800, a sum given annually between 1944 and 1946. The grants gradually fell to £1,600 in 1947, then £600 for the next five years, rising again to £1,600 in 1955, by which time the donations had been re-designated for International Service. In the First World War Joseph Rowntree had personally given generously to the FAU, and the Joseph Rowntree Charitable Trust gave substantial grants from 1939 onwards, on the grounds – noted in their minutes – that "it will probably be much more difficult to raise necessary money this time."

During the Second World War Paul Cadbury was in his mid- to late 40s. Only a man of his energy and ability could have sustained the pace and variety of work that he undertook. As his son Charles recalled, he attended weekly board meetings at Bournville; ran the sales and marketing departments of Cadbury with a much-depleted workforce; served on the Birmingham City Council and its committees; began the planning for the rebuilding of Birmingham after the war; and worked as an air-raid warden. When his daughter Margaret was ill with pneumonia or other complications associated with her cerebral palsy, he would undertake the night shift, so that his wife and the child's nurse could sleep. Organising the FAU was somehow fitted in with these other commitments. Paul would drive furiously into the yard of Manor Farm on his motorbike, would inspect progress and then deal quickly with any questions of discipline or organisation. His experience from the First World War meant that he was familiar with all stages of the Unit's work, from transporting ambulances to the battlefront to preparing for major operations on the severely wounded men once they were evacuated.

Nor were the issues of deployment and conduct straightforward. To be consistent with Quaker principles and practice, responsibilities in the FAU could be changed and reassigned, in theory without ill-feeling, on the basis of the shared views of a meeting of participants. There were also real doubts about persevering with the Unit, after it only narrowly managed to extricate itself from the early *débacles* of the war. As Tegla Davies recorded, "Finland and Norway added evidence to the tale, as Greece would do later, that it only needed the FAU to enter a country for it to capitulate forthwith." But, as with other theatres of the war, the Unit steadily increased in credibility and effectiveness. Invaluable work was done, not only in areas of fighting, but among communities affected by the war, including people in Egypt, Lebanon, Syria, Sicily and then mainland Italy.

The Red Cross and Friends' Ambulance Unit badge from Rachel Wilson's First World War nursing uniform.

In his history of the FAU, Davies draws several striking conclusions. Much of the ultimate value and success of the Unit could be attributed to a Quaker acceptance of discipline and training, he affirms. He also concludes that it was a "tribute to the essential tolerance and broad-mindedness of the British people and its Government, even in the darkest days of the War." Those who served in the Unit rarely met with anything but courtesy and helpfulness when dealing with government officials and army officers.

Immediately after the Second World War, Barrow Cadbury renewed his efforts to advance the cause of greater understanding between nations, in the quest for lasting peace. This was a time when the Yearly Meeting of the Society of Friends and their Meeting for Sufferings rearticulated the moral case for disarmament and opposition to conscription. In 1946 Barrow wrote to Ernest Bevin, Labour Secretary of State for Foreign Affairs, about arms reduction; and to his Conservative successor at the Foreign Office, Anthony Eden, about achieving improved relations with Russia. Not to have done so would have been a betrayal of his lifelong beliefs.

The annual donations of several hundred pounds from the Barrow Cadbury Fund to Lansbury's Embassies of Reconciliation, which continued throughout the war, were transferred to the Barrow & Geraldine S Cadbury Trust and substantially increased. Between 1946 and Barrow's death in 1958, the Trust contributed £10,500 to this cause. During the same period a further £9,500 went to the Fellowship of Reconciliation, an organisation founded by an English Quaker, Henry Hodgkin, in 1915 and which continues to devote itself to the resolution of conflict by the united efforts of people of many faiths.

Perhaps as a result of Paul Cadbury's direct experience of warfare and its casualties, his trust subscribed annually to charities devoted to helping the individual victims of conflict, including the British Limbless Ex-Service Men's Association and the Ex-Services Mental Welfare Society. He also consistently supported the voluntary and community organisation known as Toc H, which had started as a soldiers' club in Belgium in 1915. Talbot House, shortened to its initials and then, in soldiers' radio signal parlance, to Toc H, was founded by an army chaplain, Reverend Philip Byard ('Tubby') Clayton, in a rented hop-merchant's premises in Poperinge, a few miles behind the trenches around Ypres. The house became a refuge and an oasis of sanity for both officers and troops. It was equipped with a library and kitchen, a beautiful walled garden and a chapel in the attic hop-loft, which was known as the 'heart' of the house and where many soldiers received their first, and often their last, communion.

After the war, Tubby Clayton opened Toc H hostels in London, to house men coming to the capital in search of work. As the residents often contributed in some way to the local community, the hostels rekindled the original spirit of fellowship and service, and the movement spread rapidly across the world during the 1930s. Many Toc H men went to work in the leprosy colonies of Africa, and it was also one of the first organisations to back the National Blood Transfusion Service. The Paul S Cadbury Charitable Trust made annual donations to Toc H well into the 1970s, and from 1969 contributed £50 every year to the Friends Ambulance Unit Members' Assistance Fund for at least a decade. Paul Cadbury's preoccupations were different from those of his father, and show how priorities changed as one generation succeeded another.

Chapter 6
A New Professionalism

At the end of the Second World War, Paul Cadbury was sustaining a remarkable level of work across many different spheres. He was chairman of Birmingham's Research Committee, which produced a publication entitled *When We Build Again* in 1941, a vision of a better future for the city of which he was so proud, written during the very darkest days of the war. As honorary secretary of the West Midland Group on Post-War Reconstruction and Planning, he steered through several influential reports, including *Conurbation: A Planning Survey of Birmingham and the Black Country* in 1948. His own book, *Birmingham 50 Years On*, was published in 1952. By then he was an acknowledged authority on the effective organisation of local authorities, and consequently was appointed to the Royal Commission on Local Government in the Greater London Area, on which he served from 1957 to 1970.

Paul Cadbury's plan for a new Civic Centre in Broad Street, Birmingham, envisaged for the year 2002, in his post-war book entitled Birmingham 50 Years On.

During this period Paul was also developing the sales and marketing departments at Cadbury, on which the post-war success of the business depended. He may well have been encouraged to undertake such a variety of public work by the fact that his cousin Laurence Cadbury remained in post as company chairman until 1959, with Paul serving as vice-chairman. His own period as chairman, from 1959 to 1965, was relatively short and he retired at the age of 70. A full decade before he took up the chairmanship, he was awarded the CBE for outstanding services to the Ministry of Food.

What these activities demonstrate is Paul's complete identification with the role of central and local government in the pursuit of improving housing, planning and reconstruction. The West Midland Group on post-war planning worked assiduously on their report *Local Government and Central Control*, published in 1956, and in recognition of this Paul was invited to serve on the Central Housing Advisory Committee the following year. He also applied his political influence to strengthen the preservation of the green belt on Birmingham's southern and western boundaries, at the same time using the Barrow & Geraldine S Cadbury Trust to bring further protection to parts of the Birmingham greenbelt. He funded a third of a three-year fellowship at Birmingham University on 'The Location of Industry' from his own trust. His donations were never intended to be a substitute for the government action with which he was personally identified, but they could strengthen it in areas that might otherwise struggle for funds.

Children collecting eggs at Chapmans Hill School Farm, on the south-west edge of Birmingham.

Chapmans Hill School Farm, set up by Paul in 1972 as a joint venture with Birmingham City Council for visits by urban schoolchildren, was rapidly oversubscribed. The annual report for the Barrow & Geraldine S Cadbury Trust and Paul S Cadbury Trust in September 1973 noted of the farm:

> *The education expenditure was met entirely by the City of Birmingham's Education Committee. The [Cadbury] Trusts paid for the conversion and renovation of the buildings with an educational purpose in view, and supplied the working capital for the farm, as well as the farm manager's salary. (This expenditure was offset by income from farm produce.) The full-time teacher's salary, educational equipment, and costs of travel (about ten miles from the city centre) were met by the City, which also handled appointments and arrangements for school visits. The Farm was the subject of favourable publicity, and was a project of national significance.*

Between 1973 and 1975 Chapmans Hill School Farm received £21,000 from the Barrow & Geraldine S Cadbury Trust and £8,400 from the Paul S Cadbury Trust. The farm was on the edge of a country park – purchased by Paul's trust – and provided a nature trail and views over much of Birmingham and Worcestershire.

Post-war politics and the creation of the Welfare State meant that substantial expenditure by the Cadbury trusts for which Paul was responsible could be diverted from many of the institutions previously supported by his parents, Barrow and Geraldine. With hospitals, schools and remand homes now the acknowledged responsibility of the State, the list of grants from Barrow and Geraldine's trusts shows funds being redirected to causes which would otherwise be unsupported in the new social order. The Quaker Selly Oak colleges at Westhill and Woodbrooke, in Birmingham, still received substantial sums: £3,200 and £2,600 in 1957 and 1958 for the former, for example; and during the same period regular annual payments of about £500 were made for the latter, all from the Barrow & Geraldine S Cadbury Trust. Payments from the Barrow Cadbury Fund included a generous annuity to Dr James Rendel Harris, the first director of studies at Woodbrooke, and through the 1940s and 1950s seem to have been made to honour what were felt to be continuing obligations inherited from Barrow and Geraldine. These included £7.10.0 to "an old Gospel temperance worker"; £50 to "an old school-friend of Geraldine's"; and through the 1950s around £50 a year to the former superintendent of Uffculme Friends' Ambulance Unit Hospital. Also in receipt of financial support in her old age was Marian Priestman, who had worked very closely with Geraldine and accompanied her on visits to families with deprived children.

Meetings of the trustees of the Barrow & Geraldine S Cadbury Trust in the 1950s and 1960s were sometimes held at Bournville, but more usually were either at Paul and Rachel's house – Low Wood, 32 St Mary's Road, Harborne, just three miles from the city centre – or at his sister Dorothy's home at 21 Colmore Road, Birmingham. By 1960 Paul had ensured that the next generation of the family was being brought on to the trustee body: his daughters Catherine Hickinbotham and Philippa Southall, and his sons Edward and Charles. His younger sister Cherry, then nearing the end of her time as headmistress of Chelmsford High School for Girls in Essex, was rarely able to attend meetings until she retired and moved to Stratford-upon-Avon in 1961.

Left *Dorothy A Cadbury (1892–1987), eldest child of Barrow and Geraldine Cadbury, and trustee of the Barrow & Geraldine S Cadbury Trust from 1934 to 1987.*

Right *Geraldine M Cadbury (1900–99), youngest child of Barrow and Geraldine Cadbury, and always known in her family as 'Cherry'. She served as a trustee of the Barrow & Geraldine S Cadbury Trust from 1934 to 1994, when she resigned after sixty years' service.*

At the meeting on 3 April 1960, the main item of business was penal reform. The trustees received a report on discussions with Frank Foster of the Borstal After-Care Association. Frank had started his career as a probation officer in Birmingham, where he had encountered Geraldine Cadbury. She had had reason to rap him over the knuckles on one occasion, but she did it with considerable tact and in such a way that thereafter he regarded her with a mixture of awe and gratitude. Frank was a small man, with great energy and assertiveness, and was grappling with the problem of what to do with ex-Borstal boys. Contact with the Cadbury family and their trusts had been made on the recommendation of the Permanent Under-Secretary at the Home Office, Sir Charles Cunningham, after an exploratory meeting with Paul.

The outcome of these discussions was that a specially equipped hostel was established in north London, so that young men who had been released from Borstal could be given the opportunity to adjust to a more normal life and would not immediately re-offend. It was called the Southfield Experiment, and was largely funded by the Southfield Trust, which held funds transferred specifically from the Barrow & Geraldine S Cadbury Trust. Four of Paul's children – Catherine, Edward, Charles and Philippa (as chairman) – served as its trustees. For the first five years the Southfield Trust was responsible for both capital and day-to-day expenses. By the time the Home Office took over the funding of the project in 1972, nearly £50,000 had been spent by the Cadbury trusts.

The success of the Southfield Experiment encouraged the Home Office to form the Mellanby Trust, which was intended to help female offenders. Paul served on its committee, and a hostel for young women was opened in 1964. The Nuffield Foundation provided the building costs and the Barrow & Geraldine S Cadbury Trust contributed £21,360 towards running expenses. The project was a failure, however, and the verdict of Philippa Southall, one of Paul's children to be involved with it, emphatic:

> *The girlies' [scheme] was hopeless. Forget the girlies ... the ex-Borstal girls only wanted one thing and that was a baby, and when they got their baby, it wasn't a doll. End of story.*

How was Paul Cadbury remembered in his maturity? Recorded tributes to him went a long way beyond the merely respectful. His approach to management, whether of the family business or of his charitable trusts, was to be inclusive in a way that was clearly derived from Quaker practice. He spoke frequently to his directors about important decisions, but also to more junior staff, always feeling for the sense of a meeting. It was this approach that led to the choice of his cousin Adrian to succeed him as chairman of Cadbury in 1965, although Adrian was relatively young and inexperienced. Once that decision had been made, Paul knew not to interfere. One of his recommendations, used both in the office and at home, was "Well, my view is – and always has been – don't talk to the captain when he's on the bridge." Paul was also able to make light of serious issues. Sir Adrian Cadbury recalled a favourite saying of his:

> *It's no good sitting around and wishing.*
> *That never made any man great.*
> *It's God that gives the fishing,*
> *But you've got to dig the bait.*

An anonymous Quaker testimony to Paul refers to his "ability to sense almost instantly what was the essential quality of the issue under discussion; aided by a phenomenal memory, which not only recalled details of conversations held years earlier, but the outcome of the Trustees' deliberations in dozens if not hundreds of cases."

Others might have wanted to exercise strict personal control over the various family trusts, but Paul's inclination was frequently to pass responsibility to the next generation, with a clear message that not only were they to experience the exhilaration of successful projects brought to a satisfactory conclusion but also that they should learn from schemes which did not prove to be of lasting value. By the time he had passed the chairmanship of Cadbury over to Adrian, he realised that the value of the trusts' shares in the business was going to increase substantially, particularly after the merger with Schweppes in 1969. Paul had already (in 1964) appointed Edith Ferneyhough, his former secretary at Bournville, to act as a clerical secretary to both the Barrow & Geraldine S Cadbury Trust and the Barrow Cadbury Fund; and in the following year the office moved from George Road to 2 College Walk, Selly Oak, Birmingham.

Paul Cadbury's own account of the work of the various trusts, written in 1970, makes clear his commitment to several different areas of work. He gave an immense amount of time and effort to planning issues and to what would now be called environmental conservation, making generous donations to various National Trust appeals and buying properties in and around the Lickey Hills near Birmingham. He was also an enthusiastic supporter of the Ironbridge Gorge Museum Trust in Shropshire,

William Westwood, The Upper Part of Coalbrook Dale, *showing two of the eighteenth-century houses built by the Darby family of Quakers close to their ironworks at Ironbridge in Shropshire. Paul Cadbury was an enthusiastic supporter of the Ironbridge Gorge Museum Trust.*

contributing to appeals to help restore the historic Quaker houses of the Darby family and to setting up a scheme to employ young people on Community Service Orders to carry out conservation work. What he was reluctant to do was tie the younger trustees to his priorities. Instead, with a transfer of capital from the Barrow & Geraldine S Cadbury Trust, in 1961 he set up and funded the new Worgan Trust, which subsequently purchased Windmill and Waseley Hills, on the outskirts of Birmingham, in 1969. The following year Paul wrote to the clerk of Worcestershire County Council and the town clerk of Birmingham City Council:

> *On behalf of a charitable trust I have recently purchased Windmill and Waseley Hills, just under 100 acres and much of it over 900 feet above sea level. The Trustees envisage that this land may be made available for public use ... I hope that Worcestershire County Council and the City of Birmingham, who are the two planning authorities mainly concerned in the development of additional recreational facilities on the perimeter of the built-up area, will feel that this land will be suitable as a public park ... The land is at present let to farming tenants and I hope that their interests will not be overlooked.*

Opposite
Margaret Cadbury (1930–50), Paul and Rachel Cadbury's youngest child, had cerebral palsy. Her condition prompted the foundation of Carlson House School in Birmingham in 1947, built as a special school for children with cerebral palsy and funded equally by the Ministry of Health and Education and the Paul S Cadbury Trust.

The property was already bounded on the south and west sides by land belonging to the National Trust, and Paul may have considered handing the property over to them for permanent protection, but his instincts were to work through the local authorities with which he was so much identified.

Another personal commitment shared by Paul and Rachel Cadbury was to medical research, particularly in the field of cerebral palsy. Their daughter Margaret, diagnosed with this condition at her birth in 1930, died at the age of 20. They looked after her at home with the help of a team of carers, rarely leaving her on her own and taking holidays separately so that one of them could be with her. In 1947 Carlson House in Birmingham had been opened as a special school for children affected by cerebral palsy, funded in part by the Ministry of Health and Education but with half of all its capital costs being met by the Paul S Cadbury Trust. On 28 January 1970, Paul wrote to his fellow trustees to explain his future proposals for the school:

> *Since it started in 1947 this has been one of the outstanding success stories in the treatment of handicapped children. It is still a very happy ship. Recently we have been considering whether we could install a new classroom specially designed for the older severely handicapped children, where they could have a certain amount of independence. The result is a unique lay-out. In addition we propose to add on a new classroom for 5- to 6-year olds, so that the present large room can be used as a school hall ... The whole liability to the Paul S. Cadbury Trust will probably be in the region of £7,000 to £8,000.*

A.C. TATHAM.

In 1974 the future of the school was threatened by reductions in grants from the Spastics Society, but Paul was able to compensate for this by persuading the local authorities involved to increase their contributions. The Paul S Cadbury Trust then made an interest-free loan of £20,000 to the Midland Spastic Association, so that support for Carlson House School would continue.

Paul also funded, from his own trust, a series of studies into cerebral palsy conducted at Aston and Birmingham Universities. These ranged from support in 1969 and 1970 for the Neurological Children's Assessment Clinic at Birmingham University's Institute of Child Health, to a grant in 1976 towards the Speech Audiometry Project at Aston University.

Important though these initiatives were to Paul, he seems to have regarded them as a reflection of his own personal priorities, influenced by his concern for his daughter Margaret. Certainly medical research was not adopted as a long-term priority for the Barrow & Geraldine S Cadbury Trust, even though Paul himself was known to feel that if the war had not interrupted his university education, he might have pursued a career in medicine rather than manufacturing and business. As it was, of his children, Catherine married a consultant surgeon; Edward became a doctor; and Philippa read medicine at Birmingham University. Perhaps Paul concluded that the field of medical research was already supported by the vastly greater resources of the Nuffield Foundation and the drug companies, meaning that in the longer term his own family's trusts would have relatively little impact.

What seems never to have wavered was the commitment of the Trusts to penal reform. Writing in 1970, Paul described how, after Barrow's death in 1958, his children and grandchildren determined to devote substantial funds to this field, informed by the service of three of the trustees as magistrates, their involvement with an approved school, concern for delinquent children shared by successive generations, and Paul's own experience as a prison visitor. In 1969 and 1970 the Barrow Cadbury Fund supported the Winson Green Wives and Families Centre, which had been started by the Birmingham probation service to provide play facilities in a church hall opposite the prison gates. While the wives of offenders visited their husbands, the children were welcomed and supervised at the centre, which was used by over 10,000 people within its first three months of opening.

By 1968 Paul Cadbury was convinced the Trusts and the Fund were in a position to distribute such substantial sums that a part-time 'administrative secretary' was needed. His approach to the appointment was carefully considered and not what might have been expected. He and Edith Ferneyhough would continue to act as administrative chairman and clerical secretary respectively. What Paul wanted was someone with the time and experience to look critically at the way the Trusts were using their money, giving special attention to the difficult area of international peace and understanding.

In Kenneth Nicholson the trustees seemed to have found the ideal person for this role. He had previously been the headmaster of Friends' School at Saffron Walden in Essex, was the author of well-received books on aspects of education and had taken early retirement in order to have more time for writing. His interests and experience seemed an excellent match with the part-time post envisaged by Paul. He was to concern himself with the Barrow & Geraldine S Cadbury Trust and the Barrow Cadbury Fund, but not with Paul's own trust.

Children in the garden at Carlson House School in Birmingham.

On 31 October 1968 Nicholson delivered his first report. He told the trustees that he had studied the records of the Trust and the Fund, and had talked to Paul, Frank Foster and Lewis Waddilove, the secretary of the Joseph Rowntree Charitable Trust, whose offices in York he had visited. There had, however, been an unexplained setback. Edith Ferneyhough had been absent when he arrived and had indicated that she wanted to be replaced as soon as possible, although she was willing to act as an adviser. In spite of having to manage without well-informed and experienced secretarial support, Nicholson was able to write a succinct account of previous Trust policy – and make suggestions on where it might be directed in future.

He noted from a survey of Trust expenditure in 1963 that the priorities fell into three broad areas. Roughly the first third of expenditure went to social research and penal reform, which was exactly as Barrow and Geraldine Cadbury would have wished. The second third was directed towards education, particularly Friends' schools, again continuing the original purposes of the Trust. The final third was devoted to causes associated with the Society of Friends and a large number of small donations and subscriptions. Nicholson continued, "Obviously the Trust could spend its money differently. It could concentrate on Youth Work or Social Work. Instead it gives most generously to the Society of Friends, to Education, and to Penal Reform and Research."

He himself was thoroughly familiar with the needs of education, remarking that "Educationalists have at least one thing in common – an ability to devise ways of keeping abreast of progress by continuing to need money." He was on relatively unfamiliar ground with penal reform but undertook to research the sector, which was attracting such substantial grants, including £3,000 from the Barrow & Geraldine S Cadbury Trust to the Cambridge University Institute of Criminology in 1967.

Nicholson's three conclusions were welcomed by the trustees. He said that the things that impressed him most were:

(i) The really important work (e.g. Southfield...) which has been and is being supported, often anonymously by Trust and Fund;
(ii) The way in which the Trustees, or representatives of the Trustees, maintain a personal interest in what is going on – an interest that in its way is clearly valued as much as the original financial support.

His third point was to note an unease among trustees over the large number of small grants given to projects concerned with 'Peace and International Relations'. "It would be most easy to spend wastefully in this field," he noted, "and I have no inclination to rush in with suggestions." Instead he outlined a programme of investigation to help the trustees navigate these hazardous waters.

The trustees, and Paul in particular, clearly felt that they had appointed an administrator who would bring greater professionalism to the work of the Trust and the Fund. It was with real sadness that on 16 March 1969 – just six months after his appointment – Paul had to report the sudden and unexpected death of Kenneth Nicholson. The trustees immediately decided that the educational expenses of his son Nigel at Leighton Park – Paul Cadbury's old school – would be met either from the Barrow & Geraldine S Cadbury Trust or the Barrow Cadbury Fund. The following week, on 25 March, Paul presented a memorandum to the trustees which began by saying that Nicholson's death was a tragedy:

> *We have lost a personal friend of great quality and an administrator who was exactly what we had hoped for ... He has shown us how an able and concerned Friend can contribute to the very difficult and onerous job of spending money wisely.*

Characteristically, Paul did not propose to appoint someone who would replicate the strengths that Nicholson had brought to the post of administrative secretary, grateful though they were for the way he had "shown them the way" and given an "inspiring lead". Instead he saw an opportunity to build on Nicholson's brief but significant contribution by moving in new and different directions.

Chapter 7
'Fewer and Larger'

If Barrow Cadbury set up and shaped the trust that is still named after him, it was Paul Cadbury, more than anyone else, who made it what it is today. He did so through a number of crucial decisions made between the autumn of 1968 and the summer of 1969, less than a year later. Those months saw not only two appointments of lasting significance but also a radical review, instigated by Paul, of the purposes of the Trusts and Fund.

There were other factors. In 1969 Paul was 74; far from wanting to take things easy, following his retirement as chairman of Cadbury four years earlier, he now devoted all of his still considerable energies into reshaping and re-equipping the Barrow & Geraldine S Cadbury Trust. It became, after the welfare of his family, his greatest concern and preoccupation. His daughter Philippa, who with her husband Stephen used to join her parents on two-week holidays, remembered her mother saying:

> *It's alright for the first ten days. After the first ten days, he's thinking about the Board meeting and he ought to be back here ... When he retired, I thought "That's wonderful, we shall have a fortnight without any of this". Not at all. After ten days he started worrying about the Trust.*

Then there were the implications of the Cadbury merger with Schweppes, first proposed in 1968 and completed in 1969. The assets of the Trusts increased dramatically, as Paul had predicted. In 1960 the Barrow & Geraldine S Cadbury Trust had capital, in Cadbury shares, of £1,157,992 and distributed £82,443 in grants. Ten years later in 1970 – and after the merger – its capital amounted to £4,377,978 and its grants to £180,960. By 1980 the value of its capital was £5,989,833 and £492,004 was paid out in grants. Paul was determined to ensure that the resources of the Trusts and the Fund were used to maximum effect, in the areas which he and his parents had identified as particularly needing and deserving help.

Paul's memorandum to his fellow trustees of March 1969 showed how far his thinking had moved in the space of a few months, and particularly since the death of Kenneth Nicholson. Having praised the attributes that had proved so valuable, Paul wrote:

> *We shall not find anyone with just his qualities. In fact I do not think we should try to do so. His mature outlook was invaluable to me, but for the future well-being of the Trusts we need a younger man ... I want to keep prominently before Trustees the importance of a well-structured organisation ... As long as I can continue as Administrative Chairman I should expect to act as 'Chief Officer' with a younger Executive Secretary working under me. The rest of the team could consist of two or three experts in the particular fields in which we are interested. For example (the list is only given to illustrate the point and is not exhaustive):-*
>
> 1. *Religion – particularly Quakerly concerns.*
> 2. *Education – e.g. the handicapped.*
> 3. *Penal Research and Reform.*
> 4. *Peace and International Understanding.*
> 5. *Town and Country Planning.*

What he envisaged was an organisation with a full-time executive secretary, supported by one or two part-time staff with relevant experience, who would not necessarily live in Birmingham and who, with the benefit of expert advice from people eminent in their field, might be willing to advise without a fee, but with their expenses paid. He concluded by saying that, since Nicholson's death:

> *I have been thinking almost continuously of the future administration here. I have scribbled out what appears in this memorandum at odd times ... When I know how far our minds are running on similar lines, I shall feel much more confident in going forward with a plan.*

For the plan to work, the appointment of an outstanding executive secretary was essential. There are two accounts of how Anthony Wilson came to be appointed to this post, however. Catherine Hickinbotham's recollection was that her father was contacted by a highly regarded Quaker academic, Professor Roger Wilson, who asked him if he knew of any opportunities for the employment of his son Anthony, who was near the end of a term with the civil service in Malawi in Africa. Anthony Wilson's own explanation is that he met Lewis Waddilove, the director of the Joseph Rowntree Memorial Trust from 1946 to 1979, during a tour of Africa in 1965. They spent the evening together, during which Anthony asked him if there was any chance of a job with the Rowntree Trust. Waddilove had to tell him that there was not. On his return home, Waddilove was telephoned by Paul Cadbury, whom he knew well from service together in the Friends' Ambulance Unit, to ask whether he knew of a suitable successor to Kenneth Nicholson. Waddilove mentioned the

idealistic young man whom he had met a few weeks before. That both accounts may be true seems to be borne out by Paul's note to the trustees:

> *When we appointed Kenneth Nicholson we knew that Anthony Wilson (Roger's son) might be a suitable candidate, but he was not then available. This morning I have received a very private letter from Lewis Waddilove telling me that Anthony will be looking for a job quite soon and would like one with an organisation having an interest in overseas work. He (with his wife and family) has been the Social Development Officer to the Malawi Government for five or six years. He has excellent academic qualifications – P.E.P. at Oxford and Social Anthropology at Manchester. I propose to see him.*

What is certain is that the appointment was not made with quite the open competition expected today.

Opposite
A watercolour of Moor Hall Farm, the country home of Paul and Rachel Cadbury.

The next step was considerably more idiosyncratic. First Paul invited Anthony to an interview in his office, which went well. Anthony and his wife were then asked to lunch at Paul's country house, Moor Hall Farm, and told to arrive at twelve o'clock. The timing, it transpired, was crucial. On the doorstep, Anthony was given a fishing rod and was told to catch two trout from the pool by the house for lunch, while his wife Anne was interviewed by Paul and Rachel Cadbury. "I don't know if I got the job because I caught the fish, or Anne passed the interview," Anthony surmised.

In making the appointment, in June 1969, Paul was consciously giving Anthony the opportunity to put international affairs high on the Trust's priorities. He was also distancing the Trusts from what was usual practice in similar charities. At that time there was no accepted standard or ethos for running a charitable foundation. Anthony had Lewis Waddilove to turn to for advice, and he in turn introduced him to a group of trust executives, who called themselves the "Donors' Dozen" and met together at regular intervals. Most were retired admirals and generals, former ambassadors or distinguished academics. In that hierarchy, Anthony reckoned that, with his ex-colonial civil service background, he ranked as "Administrator 4th Class".

The "Donors' Dozen" gave Anthony a model of what he wanted to avoid in his role. He was determined to build relationships which were not based on paternalism, or on the sense of power that can gradually corrupt the distribution of money to deserving causes. Anthony was also aware that his period of service in Africa was not a passport to acceptance by the immigrant community in Birmingham, rather the reverse. He had to tell Paul Cadbury, after two or three introductions when his African experience was mentioned, "Look ... working for an imperial government in a colonial situation in Africa is *not* a good introduction, whatever my motivations were. We went to Malawi because we wanted to work under an independent government ... But that is not the way to introduce me."

Sometimes Anthony's proposals to the trustees for improving international relations involved small amounts of money and a disproportionately significant return. In 1971 Hugh Foot, the former colonial administrator and diplomat enobled as Lord Caradon in 1964 (the year he was appointed as British Ambassador to the United Nations), approached Paul Cadbury with a quandary. Although Lord Caradon had retired in 1970, he was still actively engaged in the problems of international violence and poverty, and had also attended Leighton Park, the Quaker boarding school where Paul had been educated, albeit he was 12 years younger. Caradon's discussions with Paul revolved around the obstacles to a peaceful settlement of the First Sudanese Civil War, which had raged since 1955 between the northern-based government and the Anyanya separatist movement in the south of the country. Both sides were crippled by internal ethnic divisions, factionalism and instability, with the added complication of the southern rebels being armed by the Israelis, as Anthony Wilson discovered on a reconnaissance visit to the region, when he was taken to an arms depot.

Following Lord Caradon's approach to Paul Cadbury, Anthony met Mading de Garang, one of the Anyanya leaders in exile in Britain, who persuaded him that if the heads of the various warring groups could be brought together, there was the possibility of a peace agreement. Funding from any government source would have been difficult and time-consuming to secure, so the trustees agreed to pay for air tickets to fly half a dozen key figures, scattered around Africa and Europe, to talks in Addis Ababa. The costs of the flights amounted to about £700, and were paid for by the Barrow Cadbury Fund. The result was the Addis Ababa Accord of March 1972. The Fund also paid the legal expenses of employing Sir Dingle Foot QC, brother of Lord Caradon, to represent the Anyanya rebels, now unified into the Southern Sudan Liberation Movement, at the successful talks with the government. The fighting came to an end in 1972, and by the following year the Barrow Cadbury Fund's expenditure in Sudan was approaching £6,000, with future commitments to research into conflict and mediation.

With encouragement from Paul, Anthony Wilson visited southern Sudan in 1972. The trip was planned partly to assess the improving situation on the ground, but was also to help Anthony come to terms with his departure from long-term work in Africa. His friend, the former exile Mading de Garang, had now become the Minister for Social Services and Anthony had the opportunity to influence affairs there through the work of the Trusts and Fund. Between 15 and 30 July 1972, he travelled extensively around the country, meeting political leaders and observing the gradual return of refugees to their own villages. Once back in Britain he had further meetings with staff at the Sudanese Embassy and wrote a long report addressing issues such as the problems of urban youth, crime and social hardship, support for refugee families, orphanages and the training of probation officers.

A decade later, in the early 1980s, the Barrow & Geraldine S Cadbury Trust used relatively small grants to help shape the future of South Africa. Anthony was in close touch with Donald Woods, a white South African journalist and anti-apartheid activist who had fled the country in 1977. Woods had explained the importance of Mrs Winnie Mandela's monthly visits to her husband Nelson Mandela, at that time imprisoned on Robben Island. Winnie herself was living as an exile outside the port city of East London. The trustees of the Barrow & Geraldine S Cadbury Trust agreed to meet the costs of her flights from there to Cape Town, amounting to about £5,500 per annum, and to be continued for at least two years. In the knowledge that this source of regular funding had to be kept completely confidential if the visiting rights were not to be suspended, the payments were made through the Lincoln Trust, a charitable organisation set up to support Donald Woods following his escape from South Africa. As the agenda note for the trustees' meeting on 7 October 1984 explained, "These visits have a political as well as humanitarian aspect. Maintaining contact with Nelson Mandela provides a source of hope for the black population."

One application that caused the Trust a great deal of heart-searching concerned support for refugee camps in Mozambique, then full of young men who had fled from Rhodesia in the early 1970s. There had long been Quaker involvement in Rhodesia, with a farming project in the west of the country, and Anthony Wilson knew some of those involved in the struggle against white minority rule. One of these was Didymus Mutasa, by 2011 Zimbabwean Minister of State for Presidential Affairs and Secretary for Administration of the ZANU-PF party, who had been a student at Fircroft School of Adult Education, one of the Cadbury-funded colleges in Selly Oak, Birmingham. Mutasa was keen for Anthony to meet Robert Mugabe, on the grounds that he "was going to be *the* big man" in an independent Rhodesia. The two men came to the Trust's office at 2 College Walk, Selly Oak, and Mutasa explained the desperate need for a health programme and education in the refugee camps. Anthony recalled the conversation that took place:

> *... then Mugabe spoke, and made it very, very clear – now he must have known what he was saying – that these camps, yes, they were refuges for these people, but they were also training camps ... for the ZANU Liberation Army. And, I won't say I pressed him on this, we just talked about it, and he made it very clear that money would go into a common pot, and would then be allocated according to the needs at the time ... He knew why I was quizzing him about this, and he did not compromise in his answers. So, at the time, in my book, he was a very honourable guy to deal with. Very clear-headed and very straight, and he was not going to kow-tow in order to get money.*

The annual report for the Barrow & Geraldine S Cadbury Trust for 1975 to 1977 is a positive and confident document, but it also refers to two grants that were not made:

> *Refugees* [from Rhodesia] *in camps in Mozambique had left their homes to join the liberation army ... it was decided not to make a grant, knowing that an opportunity to develop a friendly relationship with the liberation movement had been missed.*

The other decision to refuse a grant reflected how difficult it was for the trustees to formulate grant-making policies in Northern Ireland in the mid-1970s. The Trust's report noted that in Belfast:

> *... a novel approach helping organisations to undertake community work, ... arising from the care which they gave to the families of detainees and prisoners ... came to nothing. ... the obstacles – theoretical and practical – were too great. Amongst these was an implied expectation that Trustees should openly endorse the political objectives of one of the organisations.*

There was also a longer assessment of the various ways in which the Barrow & Geraldine S Cadbury Trust, the Paul S Cadbury Trust and the Barrow Cadbury Fund could support the Peace Movement in Belfast, but which urged caution in how any grants were distributed:

> *It is important for* [the Peace Movement] *to be rooted in Northern Ireland people's experience, not English money ... Although temporary assistance was given, Trustees came to question its effectiveness: it* [the Peace Movement] *gave no credit to others who had been working before them; secondly, by accepting large sums of money, it placed itself in a position of power over local groups;* [and] *thirdly, its use of the media could place other people at risk, sometimes without their consent.*

The Ballycastle Centre at the Corrymeela Community in County Antrim: this Christian organisation is committed to working towards reconciliation between Catholics and Protestants in Northern Ireland.

The assessment concluded that, while wishing the Peace Movement well in its "self-imposed task", its future would depend "on the support – personal and financial – which it can generate in Northern Ireland, rather than from overseas well-wishers."

Gradually, and at times painfully, the Barrow & Geraldine S Cadbury Trust identified ways in which policies towards Northern Ireland could be assembled, piece by piece, in what at times seemed like a difficult and unrewarding jigsaw puzzle. There were from the outset several compensating advantages. The Quakers had been one of the very few groups to engage effectively with relief work during the Irish Hunger in the late 1840s, and their contribution had not been forgotten. Another strength was the Society of Friends' long-standing association with peace initiatives and pacifism. That in turn made it less likely that the Trust and the Fund would allow themselves to be infiltrated by the intelligence services or the paramilitaries of either side. Even so, on his visits to Northern Ireland, Anthony Wilson sometimes found himself under suspicion, with what could have been frightening consequences.

The decision to enter the troubled waters of Northern Ireland seems to have been taken by the trustees in the spring of 1971, when they encouraged Anthony to visit Belfast. He arrived there on 15 April and immediately met representatives of the Belfast Council for Social Welfare, Protestant and Catholic Encounter (PACE), the Women Together Movement, the New Ulster Movement and the Ulster Quaker Peace & Service Committee. Contacts were also made with the Student Neighbourhood Action Project (SNAP) at Stanmillis College of Education in Belfast and with the Corrymeela Community, a Christian-based organisation founded in 1965 in County Antrim. Anthony's four-day trip usefully coincided with a visit by Richard Rowntree, who was doing research on behalf of the Joseph Rowntree Social Service Trust, and the two of them were able to pool ideas.

Most of these contacts formed the basis of long-term relationships and support. The secretary of the Belfast Council of Social Welfare, Denis Barritt, was himself a practicing Quaker and the Council funded a variety of voluntary social welfare activities. It received a grant from the Barrow & Geraldine S Cadbury Trust of £500 in 1971, followed by a further payment of £3,500 "subject to satisfactory correspondence between the sponsors and AEW [Anthony Wilson]." The Student Neighbourhood Action Project received a grant of £6,000 to fund a full-time director over three years, who in turn was to encourage students to participate in urban improvement schemes in both Protestant and Catholic areas of Belfast.

'Safe Passage across Toxic Ground' – a team-building exercise at the Corrymeela Community in Northern Ireland.

The idea that the Barrow & Geraldine S Cadbury Trust should assist a centre for mothers and children visiting Irish paramilitary prisoners in the Maze Prison – modelled partly on the similar project at Birmingham's Winson Green Prison, but also continuing the long Quaker tradition of visiting prisoners – proved far more problematic. The scheme had to be non-sectarian, as far as the trustees were concerned; but one of the paramilitary organisations involved insisted on some statement of support for their political aims. A meeting was eventually proposed with representatives of the Green Cross, which worked with various prisoners' organisations including the Campaign against Strip-Searching and the Irish Political Prisoners in Europe Solidarity Campaign. The discussion was to take place in an enormous Catholic church in the Falls Road area of Belfast. The memory of that difficult encounter has haunted Anthony ever since:

> *I found this church, that was all locked up except for one small door, so you pushed on the door and found you could get in, and then you were in total darkness, except for a tiny light at the far end. ... As I walked down the church, I could hear this thump, thump, as my feet hit the floor ... There were steps at the other end ... and a back room. There were four or five women sitting there, who really put me through it, as to what the Trust thought it was doing in Northern Ireland. There was no way in which we were meeting each other. And then the men came in ... these were more people in the Green Cross, who were 'Provos'* [Provisional Irish Republican Army] *in another guise, and we went through it all again.*

Anthony felt that he did at least reach a degree of understanding with the men, if only that the gulf between their aspirations and those of the Trust was unbridgeable; but with the women "we didn't get to that understanding point." He had found the meeting a very interesting and alarming experience, concluding that "I could have been taken hostage, and nobody would have been any the wiser." When he talked it all through with Paul Cadbury, he asked that if he was kidnapped, Trust funds should not be used to secure his release. In that eventuality, Paul promised to look after his wife and children.

The efforts of the Barrow & Geraldine S Cadbury Trust, Paul S Cadbury Trust and the Barrow Cadbury Fund to ease racial tensions in Birmingham were not as hazardous as dealing with the Provisional IRA, but were not without moments of considerable tension. Prior to 1971, the Trust did not have a distinct category concerned with 'race relations'. Grants to groups which happened to have black members came under other categories, such as social services or housing and planning. By the early 1970s the trustees had come to believe that the sense of racial and personal identity assumed in Black Studies programmes or by various self-help groups was a reasonable response by black people to their situation. This did not deny the trustees' ideal of integrated communities with equal opportunities for

Rising racial tension and high unemployment led to riots in the Handsworth and Lozells area of Birmingham in 1981 and 1985. The disturbances underlined the need for continued engagement in local community projects by the Barrow & Geraldine S Cadbury Trust.

all; however, they did recognise that white society at that time was generally unwilling and unable to accept black people on terms of equality.

The trustees concluded that black groups had a series of political choices. They could accept the role prescribed to them, for instance, by being satisfied with low-status jobs; or they could join any of the various groups on the political left, which sought revolutionary solutions to capitalism's problems and saw black people among the exploited, with a particular grievance. A further option was to challenge existing institutions to accept the presence of black people, both as individuals with the same rights as the native whites and as a reminder of the vitality of other cultures besides those already in existence in the United Kingdom. The trustees' sympathies rested with this third response. They were reluctant to make grants which could serve to reinforce black people's perceptions of themselves simply as victims who deserved help as they tried to accommodate themselves to white society; and they were out of sympathy with the thinking behind the analysis and perceptions of the revolutionary groups.

Although by the 1970s Birmingham had been a major centre for immigrant settlement for nearly 200 years, the trustees were concerned that support should be available to those people and agencies involved in the most recent migrations. The Barrow Cadbury Fund was particularly important in this respect, not only because of the decision of some West Indian organisations not to apply for registration as charities, but also in terms of being able to give support to other groups awaiting registration.

Trustees of the Barrow & Geraldine S Cadbury Trust remained convinced that backing West Midlands-based projects was the most useful contribution they could make to improving race relations in this country. The Trust's report for 1973 to 1975 notes the beginning of substantial grants to the All Faiths for One Race [AFFOR] organisation, to enable it to counter the propaganda being disseminated by the National Front and to support translation services in Birmingham so that Asian language-speakers could articulate their aspirations. The Harambee Housing Association also received increasing grants, year after year, as did the Afro-Caribbean Self-Help Organisation. In a report to the trustees in July 1976, Anthony noted that the increase in grants for 'race relations' meant that it was the most rapidly expanding of the Trusts' areas of work. In 1971 grants in this category amounted to £9,022; in 1972 it was £22,685; in 1973 it had more than doubled to £56,274; by 1974 it was £41,041; and by 1975 the sum had shot up again to £85,074.

The Asian Resource Centre in Handsworth, Birmingham, supported by the Barrow & Geraldine S Cadbury Trust since the 1970s, provides resources and practical help for Sikhs, Hindus and Muslims, based on a policy of anti-racism, anti-sexism and non-discriminatory practices.

Much more was involved than the distribution of grants. The staff in the office and the trustees both established close working relationships with those running the various groups and organisations that were receiving financial support. This in turn involved them in interacting with the role of the police in many areas of Birmingham. As Anthony recalled, "It simply wasn't possible to work with black groups there without being drawn into the policing issue." Concern over the way the police were behaving grew as the Trust began to support the Forty Hall Road group in Handsworth, which first received grants between 1973 and 1975. It was a community of young people particularly involved in the welfare of Asian groups in Birmingham, and had a close association with the Asian Resource Centre, a secular organisation which brought together Sikhs, Hindus and Muslims as well as addressing gender and other divisive issues.

At that time, the Charity Commission would not accept that improving race relations was a charitable activity, influenced partly by the insistence of such groups that they had to be free to engage in political activity. The solution for the trustees was to use the Barrow Cadbury Fund Ltd to help them, rather than the charitable resources of the Trusts. When the organisers of these and other groups were detained by the police, Anthony Wilson was ready to accompany them to the police station and provide a character reference:

> *I had to go to court and give evidence ... as far as I was concerned, it was all part of the job; if you'd made people grants, you stuck by them, and the police were pretty indiscriminate in who they would sweep up. Paul Cadbury found it very hard to grasp that the police could act like this; very, very hard to comprehend. It was just way outside his experience. And I had to lay it to him pretty strongly, that is what these guys were experiencing in Handsworth ... I was always very careful; I always kept a hot-line to the police, so I could talk to them as well; but I was there because of my links with the black groups. And Paul Cadbury swallowed quite hard, but he accepted this.*

As well as venturing into new and difficult areas of work, Paul and Anthony began a careful but radical pruning of some of the regular annual donations, which had been made since Barrow Cadbury's chairmanship. After he had been in post for two or three years, Anthony suggested to Paul that the Barrow & Geraldine S Cadbury Trust needed "to clear the undergrowth of all these subscriptions." It was a very large and eclectic collection of good causes, who regularly wrote to the Trust and just as reliably received a modest cheque in response. One example can serve for many. Every year, a cheque for two guineas had gone to the Railway Temperance Association. The cause was close to Barrow Cadbury's heart for two good reasons: like most good Victorian non-conformists he loved the railways, and like all good Quakers, he believed in temperance. There must have been a letter from the secretary of the Railways Temperance Society in the 1920s, and in the 1970s they were still receiving their two guineas. They were worthy people and Paul was concerned that they should be handled tactfully. "This is how we deal with it," he told Anthony. The charity or organisation was promised that their grant would continue for three years in some cases, and five in others. There would then be a 'thank you very much and goodbye letter'.

This process of pruning made it easier to deal with the main grant programmes. Provided applicants were efficient in their submissions, grants were paid on time and undertakings honoured. The Trusts' officers were a small, integrated body operating in what would today be called a 'shallow pyramid' structure. All the members of staff were 'secretaries'. Anthony Wilson never let himself be called director, remaining always as executive secretary. When Eric Adams joined in 1972, partly to help with the reorganisation of annual subscriptions dating back to the early 1920s, but also to help spend the rapidly growing surplus of income, he was appointed deputy secretary. There was also a finance secretary. One of the things that united them all was the agreement with trustees that they were going to be a grant-making trust. "That was our professional specialism," Anthony maintained, going on to insist:

> *We were not a researching trust; not a publishing trust ... in so far as what we were doing was worthy of research, other people would be very welcome to come and do it, we would collaborate with them. In so far as any outright lobbying ... was concerned, we would be happy to make a Barrow Cadbury Fund grant for other people to do it.*

In the 1970s the intention was that grants should be a liberating force, not a controlling mechanism for the applicants. The staff were, however, encouraged to take risks if they believed that an applicant had integrity, drive and a conviction that the project concerned had potential value. From the moment that he was appointed, Anthony Wilson was given his head by Paul Cadbury:

> *I can see now that he let me make a number of mistakes, which didn't matter, but they were mistakes. I can see that afterwards. But he was able to judge that, if I made them, it wouldn't matter.*

On 7 October 1984 Paul Cadbury chaired his last meeting of the Barrow & Geraldine S Cadbury Trust. On 24 October he died as the result of a severe stroke. At the next trustees' meeting on 9 December, his chairmanship of 26 years was remembered with a period of silent worship. His eldest daughter Catherine Hickinbotham was then confirmed as chairman of both the Barrow & Geraldine S Cadbury Trust and the Paul S Cadbury Trust. She was already chairman of the Barrow Cadbury Fund Ltd.

Paul Strangman Cadbury CBE (1895–1984), second child and only son of Paul and Rachel Cadbury; trustee of the Barrow & Geraldine S Cadbury Trust from 1934 and its chairman from 1958 until his death in 1984.

A new pattern of working had to be agreed, the upshot of which was that Catherine would drive over from her home in Leicester to the Trusts' offices one day a week. The other trustees also agreed that "when it appears that the size, urgency and importance of an application demands immediate action, in an area where Trust policy is not precise, the office and chairman will consult as necessary." In practice the change of chairman was a remarkably smooth transition, because Paul had prepared for it so carefully. Under Catherine, the same broad areas of policy were pursued and the process of pruning smaller grants was continued, under the label of 'Fewer but Larger'. At her first meeting in her new role, the categories for the Trusts' funding were listed as:

Peace and International Relations
Race Relations
Education (including Chapmans Hill School Farm)
Penal Affairs (including Southfield)
Social Services
Housing, Land and Community Planning
Employment
Health and Handicap
Minority Arts Programme
... and the Barrow Cadbury Fund Ltd 'personal grants'.

There had been a subtle re-ordering of some areas of work, but the continuities are at least as striking as the shifts in priorities.

Chapter 8
New Circumstances, New Opportunities

The dedication of Andrew Chandler's *Piety and Provocation: a Study of George Bell, Bishop of Chichester* (2008) reads: "For Eric Adams: Patron, ally and friend." That expression of gratitude and affection, felt strongly and personally, would have been echoed by many of those involved in the organisations helped by the Barrow Cadbury Trust: by the Fermanagh Trust in Northern Ireland; by those running the Community Organising Programmes which Eric nurtured; by arts organisations such as SAMPAD; by the George Bell Institute; and by many more. During the years that Eric worked as assistant secretary, from 1972 to 1993, and then as secretary of the Barrow Cadbury Trust from 1993 to 2001, he quietly but resolutely developed a range of initiatives of lasting significance, whilst at the same time forging friendships that were also greatly valued.

The appointment of Eric Adams says much for Paul Cadbury's perception that the Trusts and Fund needed a balanced professional team. In Anthony Wilson he had a secretary of exceptional energy and flair, able to operate on the world stage, confident about confronting a chief constable one moment and an unscrupulous journalist the next; or even Robert Mugabe and the Provisional IRA, if necessary.

When Anthony retired in April 1993, the Barrow Cadbury Trust laid on an unusual party for him in the George Cadbury Hall at the Selly Oak Colleges in Birmingham. It took the form of his own version of the radio programme *Desert Island Discs,* in which he selected eight records which illuminated stages of his life. His final choice, and the record Anthony would have taken if allowed only one, was Beethoven's 7th Symphony. It must have seemed an appropriate evocation of Anthony's drive, dynamism and occasionally frenetic approach to the challenges and opportunities facing the Barrow Cadbury Trust, in which *Presto – Assai meno presto* is succeeded by *Allegro con brio.* The symphony was dubbed by Wagner "the apotheosis of the dance", and around Anthony there was often a whirlwind of activity.

If one was looking for a musical analogy for Eric, it might be one of Beethoven's late string quartets: more intimate, with periods of deep reflection, episodic passages of humour and the lightest of touches to relieve the underlying seriousness of intent. Paul Cadbury sensed this early on and said to Eric, "I do enjoy, you know, having time with you. We can have a laugh, can't we? And what *does* beer really taste like, Eric?" It was Eric who was chosen to act as secretary to the Paul S Cadbury Trust following Paul's death in 1984.

Eric's background was very different from Anthony's. In 1972 he was working in a Social Services department in Worcestershire, and the pressures on him and his colleagues were immense. The Seebohm Report on Local Authority and Allied Personal Social Services of 1968 had led to a complete reorganisation and signalled the end of long-established specialism in social work. At the point when two former mental welfare colleagues had had to seek treatment themselves in psychiatric hospitals, Eric decided to look for a job elsewhere. He noted an advertisement for a post with the then Barrow & Geraldine S Cadbury Trust, and decided to apply. He knew members of the Cadbury family through the Leicester Quaker Meeting, where he had met Friends who had helped him become a conscientious objector and so avoid military conscription. Eric had also visited Paul and Rachel Cadbury's house when his son had attended a Quaker children's gathering there.

The critical moment of his interview for the post of assistant secretary came with the 'Eskimo Test', presented by Paul:

> *You realize the job could be very demanding? For example, Quakers at the moment are very concerned about the situation facing the Eskimos. Now, if we had to do something in that field, would you be prepared to go off to the far north and see what you could do about it?*

Eric was very deliberate in his response and said that he would be prepared to do what was required. When recollecting this interview, he added "And I ended up, for the first ten years of my work, in Lower Gornal, Upper Gornal and points north to Bloxwich!" (All parts of the Birmingham or Walsall conurbations in the West Midlands.) The reality was that Anthony wanted someone to tackle issues of social deprivation on the Trust's Birmingham doorstep, which Eric was ideally qualified to do. Eskimo work was to be left to Anthony. The two men met together for a business discussion over lunch in a Selly Oak Indian restaurant, to agree terms and explore such topics as the rehabilitation of the mentally ill, NSPCC workers and battered babies, the management of voluntary agencies and the role of the Society of Friends in social work. Anthony's wife Anne concluded that they would make good colleagues; and so Eric started work on 1 March 1972.

In his early years with the Trusts and Fund, Eric was content to work in a relatively unobtrusive way, to the extent that on one occasion Philippa Southall said to Anthony that she was a bit concerned that the assistant secretary was not getting his share of the limelight at Trust meetings. This was certainly not what Anthony wanted. For Eric, however, this tendency had distinct advantages: "By the time they'd talked about all Anthony's vital issues, most of mine went straight through."

What rapidly became apparent was that both the skills and the styles of Anthony Wilson and Eric Adams were complementary. Anthony brought his knowledge of international issues to the work of the Trusts, and to many of the most difficult issues in Northern Ireland and Birmingham. Eric's role was to address a wider variety of community issues, which were best dealt with in a patient, step-by-step way. "My role was the local stuff," Eric recalled, "and that suited me fine. I had a young family, and in spite of my offer to go to Lapland, I was very happy with Bloxwich."

Over the next decade, Eric gave much of his time to what was then called 'Neighbourhood Development'. The issue was another of Paul Cadbury's concerns and he wrote about it in a memorandum of 26 January 1976, prior to a trustees' meeting:

> *As an interesting development in the office, we are considering a series of small experiments in the field of community development which would be confined to the Birmingham area. Some of these are being suggested by Eric, and I have a scheme in which I am personally interested, connected with the Metchley Play Area.*

He proposed to set aside £1,000 from the Paul S Cadbury Trust, to be drawn on whenever Eric wished to support a local project, without the need of formal approvals but with details given in a report at agreed intervals. It was an approach which Paul was already using to assist overseas students studying at various Birmingham colleges and universities, and to support summer holiday play schemes. As he noted, these were things "done automatically in a village but ... slow to get off the ground in urban communities." The grants to neighbourhood schemes were often modest, but Eric believed that starting small was sensible. "A typical Quaker thing; you wouldn't leap in with a huge amount," he affirmed. As the staff of the Trusts came to know the recipients better, the size of the grant might increase with the shared confidence: "One or two didn't deliver, but very, very few."

At Anthony's instigation, Eric took on the task of trying to coordinate the work of different charities working in the same sectors in Birmingham. He met many of the staff involved and – from these contacts – brought together the West Midlands Charitable Trusts' Group. The overall aim was to strengthen civil society. Eric would quote with approval de Tocqueville's belief that "the strength of free peoples resides in the local community ... without local institutions a nation may give itself a free government, but it has not got the spirit of liberty." Of the 20 or more community development projects with which the Trusts were involved in the 1980s, one of the most effective was in Coventry. Some of its most controversial grants enabled local residents to take the city council to the High Court for breach of contract over its failure to deliver certain core services. This in turn helped to modify the attitude of council officials towards local groups. The Barrow & Geraldine S Cadbury Trust was making annual grants during this period of £1,000 to the Coventry Family Conciliation Service; £1,000 to the Coventry Resource and Information Centre; £5,600 to the Coventry Women's Information Centre; and £18,060 to the Coventry Workshop, all under the umbrella of the Coventry Voluntary Service Council.

The nature and terms of the Barrow Cadbury Fund meant that Eric, as Anthony had done before him, could make recommendations to its directors to give help to individuals as well as to the charities supported by the Barrow & Geraldine S Cadbury Trust and the Paul S Cadbury Trust. One of those whose lives were transformed by the Fund was a Polish nurse, who was introduced to Eric by Maurice Brodie, a professor at Swansea University and who was also East European. Having secured agreement from the chairman, Catherine Hickinbotham, the Fund made a grant which enabled the young woman to qualify in this country. "She married a young doctor, and now she's not only got her degree, but a PhD and her book has just gone off to be published," Eric recalled, adding that the recipient had settled in Birmingham to raise her family. Support of this sort was highly unusual, but the Barrow Cadbury Fund had the flexibility to make exceptions, and Catherine was willing to trust the judgement of her staff.

The Barrow Cadbury Fund also supported a scheme of Eric's to run a regular programme of fellowships, in memory of Paul Cadbury. The first fellow was an American called Bob Johnson, who ran a charitable foundation in Chicago and whose book *Why Philanthropy must make Democracy the first Charity* was to prove influential. Some of those subsequently receiving fellowships, such as Margaret Gallagher from County Fermanagh in Northern Ireland, went on to contribute to the

Barrow Cadbury Trust's other programmes. Another fellow was involved in community work in South Africa. "That's what I wanted the Barrow Cadbury Fund to become," Eric insisted, "it's what it should be doing."

Small-scale and often local projects were run in parallel with major national initiatives, some of them tackling difficult and contentious issues which sometimes involved fundamental disagreements with the statutory agencies, including the police. In such cases, Anthony Wilson's resilience and fearlessness were invaluable to the Barrow & Geraldine S Cadbury Trust. This was particularly the case with support for the Rape Crisis and Research Project, based in London, which received a grant of £8,500 in 1977 to enable it to provide a round-the-clock service, the first such in the country. The Trust's report for 1975 to 1977 notes that its existence is:

> *... generally welcomed by statutory agencies. The exception is Scotland Yard. Their opposition seems to be that the Project does not report all assaults to the police, as a matter of routine policy. The Trustees, who are marriage guidance councillors and GPs, as well as magistrates, argue that for the Project to do this without the consent of the victim would offend the code of confidentiality; given the low rate of conviction, and the fact that half the victims know their attackers personally, a low rate of reporting is almost inevitable.*

The staff and chairman of the Barrow & Geraldine S Cadbury Trust in 1992–93: back row from left *Pat Weaver (Finance Secretary); Dipali Chandra (Assistant Trust Secretary); Moira Westmacott (Office Secretary); Doreen Brandreth (Office Secretary); Pamela Robson (Office Secretary);* front row from left *Anthony Wilson (Trust Secretary); Catherine Hickinbotham (Chairman); Eric Adams (Deputy Trust Secretary).*

The Rape Crisis Centre also involved Anthony Wilson and the Barrow & Geraldine S Cadbury Trust in fierce exchanges with a sometimes hostile press. The fact that the Centre would not involve men in one of their functions prompted a highly critical article in the *Daily Mail,* implying that, in Anthony's words, "these mad women were anti-male." This in turn greatly upset those running the Centre. Anthony responded with characteristic vehemence:

> *I got on to the Daily Mail guy and had a long conversation with him, as to why it was perfectly reasonable for people who'd been through this experience not to want to have men around, on a particular occasion or a particular event. And after about five minutes' conversation, he came right back to the beginning again, and said: 'And why shouldn't men be there?' So I said: 'Look, you know why you journalists have got a lousy reputation? You haven't listened to a word I've said to you over the 'phone. You've got the nerve to repeat back to me your first question, and now you expect me to listen to you. I've got nothing else to say, and if you dare to carry any more reports like this, I am going to write a full account of our conversation.' Nothing else came out. That was the end of the story, completely.*

For both the trustees and for the staff of Barrow Cadbury's family trusts and fund, it was important to keep pushing at the frontiers, particularly when those confronting some of society's most intractable problems were being ignored, harassed or abused.

In 1993 Anthony Wilson retired at the age of 60. An important change in the name of the Barrow & Geraldine S Cadbury Trust also took place at this time, with chairman Catherine Hickinbotham and the trustees concluding, after consultation with Eric Adams, that Geraldine's name should be dropped from the title and that the Paul S Cadbury Trust should be absorbed into this renaming. In 1994 the two former trusts became simply the Barrow Cadbury Trust, with Eric appointed secretary of both the 'new' Trust and the Barrow Cadbury Fund Ltd. The title of his post was changed first to administrator and then, in 2000, to director. Dipali Chandra, who had joined the staff in 1989, took over the race relations brief from Joe Montgomery, who had also – since his appointment in 1986 – held special responsibility for employment and urban regeneration.

Charles Lloyd Cadbury (1926–2000), fourth child of Paul and Rachel Cadbury; trustee of the Barrow & Geraldine S Cadbury Trust from 1959 and its chairman from 1993 until his death in 2000.

In a charity with a relatively small staff, the relationship between the chairman and the executive can make all the difference to the levels of creativity and solid achievement. Both Anthony Wilson and Eric Adams had productive partnerships, initially with Paul and then with his daughter, Catherine. In 1993 Catherine was succeeded as chairman by her younger brother Charles Cadbury, and from the moment that Charles took over, his relationship with Eric was easy and fruitful. For Eric, Charles was quite simply "the best chairman I ever had, and the best boss."

One symptom of the benefits of their close working relationship was that programmes in Northern Ireland were re-energised. The situation had changed significantly since Anthony's visits in the 1970s and there was a real danger of the Barrow & Geraldine S Cadbury Trust gradually withdrawing its support and involvement. In 1986, before making a final decision, the trustees agreed that James Cadbury (or 'Jim'), the son of Paul and Rachel's eldest son Edward, and Eric Adams should make a three-day visit to Northern Ireland, looking particularly at the potential for community schemes outside Belfast. One of the first projects they visited was the Quaker Cottage, a countryside holiday, play and leisure centre for a succession of mothers and children from throughout the more strife-torn areas of Belfast. The Cottage was organised by the Ulster Quaker Service Committee, of which Jim Cadbury wrote: "They seem to have created a centre of reconciliation and industry by introducing mothers, children and young people from the local estates into a new environment of creativity."

Among the other organisations visited were the Centre for Neighbourhood Development in Belfast; the Ulster Quaker Peace Committee, who were putting together a three-year peace education committee; the Newtownabbey Women's Group; the Rathcoole Self-Help Group, also based in Newtownabbey; the Farset City Farm and Farset Community Project, Springfield Road; the Ardoyne-Alliance Playschool, which had "broken down many traditionally held stereotypes and fears"; the Corrymeela Community, which helped to run a recreation centre at Ballycastle on the Antrim Coast, but could barely raise the funds to enable Belfast children to stay there; and by no means least, the Maze Prison. The joint conclusions reached by Jim and Eric were that "the projects were well-presented, and funds in this area would be well spent." They also found that "our mere presence was so often regarded as a significant event in itself."

When the trustees considered their report, they agreed that the Trust should indeed establish a programme in Northern Ireland and that an annual budget provision of £30,000 should be made. In practice, far more than that was spent, with Jim and Eric maintaining six-monthly visits.

The Trust's commitment to Northern Ireland had been further strengthened when Charles Cadbury became chairman, and he too visited Ulster with Eric. One of the schemes which proved to be of most lasting value, and which provided a model for other counties, was the Fermanagh Trust. Here, Charles, Jim and Eric established a partnership with the departmental heads of the district council and their chief executive, Gerry Burns. The Trust then embarked on a 15-year programme in County Fermanagh, funding the restoration of former Nationalist schools which had been abandoned when the education system became increasingly polarised and had since become derelict. The Trust made large, regular

Trustees and staff of the Barrow & Geraldine S Cadbury Trust handing over a kick-start grant to the Boho Community Association in County Fermanagh, Northern Ireland, enabling the refurbishment of Boho National School as a cross-community centre. Left to right *Jim Ledwith (Fermanagh Trust); Eric Adams (Barrow & Geraldine S Cadbury Trust); Michael Tracey; Roger Hickinbotham (Barrow & Geraldine S Cadbury trustee); Charlie Farmer; Margaret Corrigan; Patsy McBrien and Anita Guy.*

contributions to set up these old schools as community centres, which adults and children of both religious traditions could use. The scheme has blossomed and led to similar programmes in Armagh and Tyrone. This continuing success Eric attributes in part to the way in which he worked with his chairman: "Charles was really a radical; he was a kindred spirit."

Both the trustees and staff of the Barrow Cadbury Trust tend to have an innate preference for letting strategic decisions emerge from the sharing of ideas, from thinking and listening. With the Cadburys, as with any family, there have been tensions and disagreements, but these have always been addressed through negotiation and accommodation, rather than explosive rows. There is something Quakerly about advancing new ideas in a way that is not personally assertive, so that the outcome seems to be a seamless consensus. This appears to be the case with the way in which the Trust reconsidered and rearticulated its response to the increasingly complex issues surrounding race and immigration.

Anthony Wilson thought deeply about the issues, as did Charles Cadbury. After Anthony's retirement Charles, as the new chairman, allowed time for the staff and other trustees to contribute to this fresh thinking. As Dipali Chandra recalled:

> *Charles was a strategic thinker. He was engaged. And he would listen to other younger trustees, in terms of their views and thinking about the direction of the Trust ... He was open to actually looking at, and understanding, the issues around the growing significance and scale of asylum. When he became chairman he was very receptive to these.*

By comparison she found Eric much less explicit, and perhaps that is part of the explanation for why the partnership between chairman and administrator worked so well:

> *Eric was tactical, in the sense that he knew the direction in which he wanted to take the Trust, and tactically how best to do that. And the strong working relationship – I think it was not just professional but personal – enabled them to move the Trust in that direction ...*

In the Trust's annual report for 1995 to 1996 there is a sense of the increasing clarity in the Trust's thinking about asylum and immigration, and of both the strategic and tactical approaches that the Trust would adopt. The report warns:

> *An Asylum and Immigration Bill is progressing through Parliament which, if enacted, will introduce draconian measures to reduce the entry of asylum seekers... A culture of disbelief and inhumanity prevails.*

The Barrow Cadbury Trust joined other funders in short-term programmes to support a range of organisations working in the field of immigration, asylum and refugee support. Asylum Aid, which provides legal representation for those fleeing persecution abroad, received funding, as did the Detention and Asylum Service. Grants were directed towards research projects on various aspects of the current appeals system. Support of £14,000 was given to the salaries of staff at the Refugee Support Centre in London, to extend their counselling and psychotherapy services. There was also a grant of £19,000 to a study being undertaken by the University of Birmingham into the mental health needs of detainees.

As chairman, Charles Cadbury also initiated reviews of other programme areas, which the trustees with special responsibility for those concerns would discuss in small, regular meetings with the administrator or the assistant administrator, Dipali Chandra. Programmes were allocated their own specific budgets, although trustees were encouraged to make the case for further allocations as needs arose. This greater discipline and professionalism was a necessary counterbalance to Eric's more intuitive and personal approach. Both he and the chairman knew they were playing to each other's strengths and enjoyed the sense of a very close partnership. If there was a possible weakness in their relationship, it was that it tended to exclude others in the organisation. Nor were these people helped to see exactly how the changing objectives of the Trust translated into their own professional objectives. Indeed, the partnership between chairman and administrator sometimes left other staff feeling like outsiders.

Since the Barrow & Geraldine S Cadbury Trust was set up in 1920, contributions to peace and reconciliation initiatives have continued to be among its highest priorities. For members of the Cadbury family who have served as trustees, as for those who have worked as members of staff or served in the Friends' Ambulance Unit, the cause of peace has been of profound importance to them; and many have registered as conscientious objectors. The pacifism of seventeenth-century Quakers has never been forgotten, however difficult it is to reconcile that ideal with the evils of twentieth-century tyranny and militarism.

The day after the German bombing of Coventry on 14 November 1940, Paul Cadbury visited the city to see the devastation and suffering for himself. After the war, German conscientious objectors set up an office in the ruins of the crypt of Coventry Cathedral, as a symbol of remorse and reconciliation. Over many years, during the 1980s and 1990s, the Barrow Cadbury Trust made annual donations of around £10,000 to support these German volunteers wishing to come to Coventry. The project was organised by the Action Reconciliation Service for Peace, which was founded in 1958 by a German, Lothar Kreyssig, to give acknowledgement of the guilt that many Germans were faced with at the end of the Nazi era, and which could be expressed through young volunteers working in countries that had suffered from German occupation or aggression.

There was a similarly long involvement with the George Bell Institute, which began with a telephone call from a young academic, Andrew Chandler. At that time he had a lectureship, on a limited tenure, in history at Birmingham University.

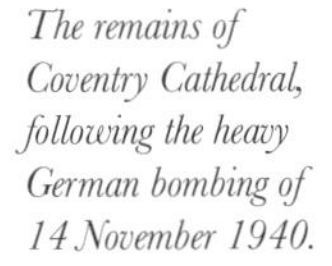

The remains of Coventry Cathedral, following the heavy German bombing of 14 November 1940.

His request was simple and direct: "I want to put on a conference with survivors of the Christian Resistance to the Nazis ... and we need a bit of money to pay for this." Eric's response was to say "Well, I'll see what I can do," and to discuss the issue with his chairman, Charles Cadbury. Almost immediately Chandler was told that he would receive a grant of £1,000 towards the conference. Eric recalled how:

> *We ended up with a wonderful conference at the University, with Eberhard Bettge, Dietrich Bonhoeffer's biographer and disciple, and Cristabel Bielenburg, author of* The Past is Myself ... *Chandler got them all there. Shirley Williams came ... and Charles and Jill, who had been very supportive.*

George Bell (1883–1958), Bishop of Chichester from 1929 to 1958. The George Bell Institute was founded in 1996 in honour of Bell and funded in part by the Barrow Cadbury Trust.

When Chandler moved to Chichester, he helped to set up the George Bell Institute in 1996, an international fellowship of scholars, writers and artists dedicated to encouraging creative work by individuals from all backgrounds and traditions, as a memorial to Bishop George Bell, who during the Second World War had – almost alone – spoken for those Germans who gave their lives for their opposition to Hitler. The Barrow Cadbury Trust report for 1997 to 1998 records a grant from the Trust of £50,000 towards the Institute's running costs. The grants continued for several years, rising to £57,500 in 1999 and £65,000 in 2000.

Writing in the report for the Barrow Cadbury Fund in 1995, Eric Adams was able to "point to a significant re-organisation of Trust programmes," in particular the allocation of special responsibilities for specific programmes to individual trustees, who were also charged with monitoring and assessing the projects receiving grants. He concluded by saying that the following words of Dietrich Bonhoeffer (the German Lutheran pastor executed by the Nazis in 1945) were apposite:

> *Do not be led hither and thither. Do and dare – not what you would, but what is right. Never hesitate over what is within your power, but boldly grasp what lies before you. Away with flight of fancy, timidity and reluctance. Out into the storm of deed and event, sustained by your faith, and freedom will receive your spirit with exultation.*

Chapter 9
Local or National?

The Cadbury family, like many other philanthropists, has had to consider whether a fairer society is best pursued by engaging with national politics and politicians; or whether more is achieved by addressing the needs of individuals and their immediate locality. There is an honourable history of Quakers doing both. Geraldine Cadbury's "patron saint" Elizabeth Fry gave practical help to the prisoners she met in Newgate Prison. But she also used her access to the crowned heads of Europe, including the kings of Denmark and Prussia, to confront them about inhumane penal institutions and the slave trade. Geraldine herself showed how both local and personal obligations could be combined with forceful access to the corridors of power. She maintained her card index with the details of every individual who had appeared before her on the bench; and was also in continual correspondence with the Home Office and attending meetings with government ministers. Immersed as they were in the history of Quaker philanthropy, she and Barrow Cadbury accepted that their charity needed to operate on both levels.

For their successors, balancing the local with the national and policy with practice would become increasingly complex. The Trust directors and trustees both recognised that issues such as racial and gender justice were changing radically. An opportunity arose in 1989 when the Trust needed to recruit a successor to Joe Montgomery, who had worked particularly on community relations in Birmingham. The secretary, Anthony Wilson, wanted to appoint someone who would broaden the Trust's experience and so help to move it in new directions. Using his contacts with various organisations that were receiving grants from the Trust, Anthony did some discreet headhunting of his own. One of those he approached was Dipali Chandra, who was working in the Department of Management Studies at Coventry Polytechnic (later Coventry University), and she was encouraged by Anthony to apply. The trustees concluded that she would help them to re-examine the Trust's approach to issues of gender and equality.

Fresh thinking was necessary, because the trustees – and particularly the secretary – recognised just how difficult it was to understand the needs of women in large parts of the Midlands when viewed from a position that was privileged. The Trust was also aware of the crucial role being played by women in the efforts to find a peaceful solution in Northern Ireland.

While she was at Coventry Polytechnic, Dipali had undertaken a year's research aimed at identifying issues faced by socially disadvantaged women. She considered how they could be helped to become self-employed, and to set up their own businesses. One practical outcome was the first Women's Enterprise Development Agency, which Dipali helped to run in its early stages. Her research also showed how the government's Enterprise Allowance Scheme – which gave a guaranteed income of £40 a week to help unemployed people establish their own businesses, and was piloted between 1982 and 1983 – could have a significant impact in the West Midlands. Joe Montgomery had already been instrumental in setting up a revolving loan guarantee fund, which ran in parallel with, and supplemented, the Enterprise Allowance Scheme. Because the loans were taken up by individuals, the Barrow Cadbury Fund (the non-charitable arm of the Trust) was used. This was an early forerunner of social investment.

Another shift in thinking was towards a more conscious commitment to racial justice. In the 1980s, and particularly after the Handsworth riots in Birmingham, the Barrow Cadbury Trust had tended to concentrate its work on reducing racial tension by supporting efforts to improve relations between different communities. By the 1990s the approach was changing significantly towards addressing issues of inequality and facilitating access to justice to those groups of people who felt that their rights were being undermined because of their race or ethnicity.

The practical ways in which the Barrow Cadbury Trust could contribute positively were through grants to organisations providing help to the most marginalised women in some of the poorest parts of the Midlands. Support was given to the Heart of England Community Foundation and to Inspire Black Country, which were encouraging local women to get more involved in community activity. The Trust also gave substantial grants to the Single Parent Action Network (SPAN), so that it could take on new staff. Its director, Sue Cohen, wrote:

> *The Trust have not only funded us, but supported us in spirit and wanted to keep the core ethos of the organisation alive. For SPAN there is an important interrelation between issues relating to gender, ethnicity, disability and class. Single parent status can encompass all of these. The Barrow Cadbury Trust is very good at seeing how separate programmes of work can dovetail together.*

Since 1996 the Barrow Cadbury Trust has regularly funded the Fawcett Society, the leading gender equality campaigning organisation, which has done much to raise awareness of women's issues, both in Parliament and more widely.

This emphasis of approach on policy matters was to have longer-term implications for the Barrow Cadbury Trust. Its work with organisations in and around Birmingham provided the Trust with first-hand knowledge of what particular communities aspired to, and clear evidence of when real progress was being made. But issues of racial and social justice had to be pursued increasingly through the government, and through the organisations that were informing its thinking and policies. One such body was the Racial Justice Committee, set up with funding from the Joseph Rowntree Charitable Trust. Anthony Wilson was a member of the committee and was later joined by Dipali Chandra, who served on it for six years. She believed that their value to the committee was partly that they brought knowledge of not only racial justice issues, but of other equality concerns as well. One of Dipali's principal contributions was to help the committee to make the connections between gender justice and racial justice. For the Barrow Cadbury Trust the two issues were also becoming increasingly intertwined.

Another sign of changing needs and priorities was the interest the Trust began to take in the Minority Arts Programme, which had been given a brief – and even terse – entry in the annual report for 1983 to 1984. The grants made that year were largely from the Barrow & Geraldine S Cadbury Trust, but with £200 contributed by the Barrow Cadbury Fund. The report notes:

> *Grants of up to £500, but usually of no more than £250, are made to ethnic minority groups or wider associations promoting minority arts. Occasionally larger grants are recommended from within the main Trust budget for projects likely to make a significant contribution to the development of Minority Arts in the West Midlands.*

The inspiration for this programme could be traced back to the support Barrow, and particularly Geraldine, gave to arts organisations and institutions in and around Birmingham. It may go back even further, to Geraldine's lifelong friendship with Winifred Oliver, whom she met as a schoolgirl at The Mount in York and who – in later life – received financial

William Holman Hunt, May Morning on Magdalen College Tower, Oxford, Ancient Annual Ceremony, c.1888–93. *The painting belonged to Richard Cadbury (1835–99) and was donated to Birmingham Museums & Art Gallery by his son and daughter-in-law, Barrow and Geraldine, in 1907.*

assistance from the Barrow Cadbury Fund. Winifred's father was a curator at the Royal Botanical Gardens at Kew, where Geraldine was invited to stay during school holidays. He was an accomplished botanical illustrator, and Winifred inherited his talents, becoming a professional painter. The fact that her path and Geraldine's took them in such very different directions seems only to have strengthened their friendship.

As so often with the initiatives of the Barrow Cadbury Trust, Paul Cadbury played a central hand in devising the Minority Arts Programme, consciously or unconsciously extending his mother's interests. In 1978 three of his grandchildren became trustees: Catherine's son Roger, Philippa's daughter Anna and Edward's son Richard. The experience was initially rather disconcerting, because their first meetings took place in their grandparents' drawing room, in which everybody sat in armchairs or on sofas, with cups of tea in their hands. It might have been easier for the new recruits if they had gathered round a formal meeting table. As Anna recalls, "I won't pretend that it wasn't extremely difficult, for some time, to speak up confidently in front of people who you'd been taught all your life were your elders and betters." Paul did, however, have his own preferred approach to induction, which was to give "the children" (then in their late 20s) "a project". For their parents he had earmarked the Southfield Trust. For the next generation, it was to be the Minority Arts Programme.

Paul's well-tried approach was to give the three new trustees absolute authority over an annual budget of £5,000 for arts activities that benefited minorities in the West Midlands. This meant that there was an agenda item to which they would speak, which in turn gave them status at the trustees' meetings. The choice of project turned out to be particularly apt, and over the next few years the sums allocated to it grew very substantially.

In the 1990s one arts programme supported by the Trust included the cost of a resident storyteller, involving a grant of £500 to West Midlands Arts. Another contributed £250 towards the Afro-Caribbean photography project at Walsall Museum and Art Gallery; and another major grant of £15,000 in 1992–93 went to South Asian Performing Arts, for the cost of launching a new initiative. One of the most enduring of these projects is SAMPAD, a leading South Asian arts organisation in England. It was founded in 1990 by Piali Ray, who wanted to provide artists working in multi-cultural Britain with the opportunity to enrich the lives of minority communities. Her aim was to foster art forms originating in India, Pakistan, Bangladesh and Sri Lanka, taking their work to schools, community groups and galleries. In 1993 SAMPAD received a grant of £8,500 towards its running costs from the Barrow Cadbury Trust.

Twenty-five years after it was founded, SAMPAD held a celebratory party at the Midlands Art Centre. By that time it had become a major force in the cultural life of Birmingham, prompting one of its funders, Arts Council West Midlands, to record:

> *What is particularly impressive about SAMPAD is its secular approach in all aspects of programming. It is artist-led in the best sense, a genuine catalyst for cultural development … valuing the 'traditional' and 'contemporary' in a new British-Asian context.*

At the anniversary party, Piali Ray singled out Eric Adams to remind him that he had been present at SAMPAD's opening event. She was able to produce a photograph showing Eric, as he recalled, "lurking in the background, trying to be inconspicuous." His role, and the contributions of the Barrow Cadbury Trust, were certainly not that. Nor were they forgotten.

Yudh *("Battle"): a contemporary British Asian dance performed by Liz Lea and Saju Hari, and choreographed at SAMPAD South Asian Arts, a Birmingham-based organisation supported by the Barrow Cadbury Trust.*

The list of other projects supported in 1992 and 1993 is a very long one and shows how, in practice, the Barrow Cadbury Trust found it difficult to move to fewer and larger grants. Recipients listed in the annual report fall into familiar categories. They begin with *Peace and International Relations* – with funding for university and academic research featuring prominently – and a total commitment of £232,646 being paid out. *Equal Opportunities* received £451,837 in grants, *Civil Rights and Social Justice* was allocated £132,216. *Penal Affairs* received a total of £118,050; *Employment* got £134,380; and *Northern Ireland,* in particular reconciliation projects, £166,670. *The Society of Friends and Other Churches* were paid £15,750; and *Policy Development and Social Services* received grants totalling £106,121. A total of £1,348,769 was disbursed during that period.

Meanwhile, the Paul S Cadbury Trust was also being used very actively during 1992 and 1993. Eric Adams spent part of 1992 on sabbatical leave in the United States with the intention that he should glean ideas that might be applicable to the West Midlands. He was particularly struck by the different forms taken by community organising in the States. On his return, and following his report to the trustees, grants of £45,000 and £10,000 were made respectively to the Citizen Organizing Foundation and its equivalent in Wales. He wrote in the annual report:

> *It is too early to say whether or how these visions will be realised, or in what form they may be fulfilled, but they are being shared with Trustees, grantees and other interested parties, and are likely to have some effect on the pattern of Trust grant-making.*

Initially not all the trustees felt included in the decision to fund the community organising programme, and perhaps among the older generation there was a suspicion of ideas emanating from North America. The younger trustees were also concerned about the amounts allocated to policies that were untried in this country. However, Charles Cadbury's trust in Eric, and his willingness to innovate, helped ensure that the Cadbury philosophy of learning from fresh ideas, even those with a risk of failure, prevailed. By 1995, £165,000 was being allocated to the programme, which supported the development of structured faith- and trade union-based social action, with the Trust continuing as one of the most loyal financial backers of the community organising movement during the subsequent decade. Over the years £4 million was to be invested. There are various strands to the community organising movement: Barack Obama trained in this method in Chicago, and in this country the current British government is investing in similar approaches.

The 1990s were also years of administrative and organisational change. Following the merger of the Trusts in 1994, there was also a very deliberate move to more formalised management structures and processes. This change was influenced in part by the professional experience that Anna Southall brought in 1996, when she became chairwoman of the Barrow Cadbury Trust and Fund. Unlike the previous two chairs, she combined the role with a demanding job. As director of the National Museums and Galleries of Wales, she was never going to be able to continue her aunt Catherine's practice of visiting the office once a week, or adopt Charles's more detached but still very accessible style of chairmanship. Nevertheless she insisted on a strictly adhered-to weekly telephone call to keep in touch between her less regular visits to Birmingham. The gradual but very deliberate moving away from Paul's practice of acting as executive chairman had, under Anna, become a clear distinction between, on the one hand, the role of chairwoman of the trustees in formulating strategy, and on the other, the responsibility of the chief executive for translating those strategies into effective projects. The transition was made easier by information technology, with the chairwoman no longer needed to sign cheques and banking done online.

The way in which the staff were managed was also addressed. Regular appraisals were introduced, to ensure that excellent performance was recognised and development needs were addressed. The introduction of new recruits to the work of the Trust was also organised more formally. A shift to a more managerial approach to staff relationships is never easy, particularly when people have worked together for many years in a close-knit, family way. To the trustees these changes were long overdue, but to Eric Adams and some of his team there seemed to be a move to unnecessary bureaucracy that went too quickly and too far. It took time for different ways of working to be accepted as an almost inevitable part of running even a small organisation.

Anna was also keen to pursue the policy of 'Fewer and Larger' grants, which had begun under Catherine's chairmanship between 1984 and 1993, but which had in practice proved very difficult to sustain. However, during the ten years between 1992 and 2002, the number of recipients of grants was reduced by half, while the amount of money being distributed doubled. In 1992 the total expenditure of what was then still the Barrow & Geraldine S Cadbury Trust was £1,348,769. By the time Charles Cadbury took over as chairman in 1993, the figure had increased to £1,507,255. Under Anna's chairwomanship, expenditure had reached £3,223,300 by 2001. At the beginning of the 1990s there were 377 grants being distributed, yet by the end of that decade the number of recipients had fallen to 228.

The policy of reducing the number of policy areas was implemented only gradually. The annual report of 1997 to 1998 still notes a total of seven programmes, with responsibilities allocated to trustees as follows:

Civil Rights (Erica R Cadbury)
Community Democracy (Charles L Cadbury)
Justice and Peace (Roger P Hickinbotham and Erica R Cadbury)
Disability (James E Cadbury)
Gender (Ruth M Cadbury)
Penal Affairs (Charles L Cadbury)
Racial Justice (Ruth M Cadbury)

The regular reviewing by the trustees of the list of programmes took place at the annual residential meetings, instigated by Anthony in 1985, shortly after the death of Paul Cadbury, and were a simple but nevertheless significant step towards a more formal and professional standard of trusteeship. They were usually held in October, with the trustees staying either at Birmingham University or in one of the Selly Oak Colleges. The meetings were to consider policy and strategy issues, and served as a measure of just how far the organisation had moved from being a reactive, grant-making family trust.

The trustees also pressed for the continuing diversification of the portfolio of investments. This process began shortly after the Cadbury merger with Schweppes and was prompted initially by a concern Anthony Wilson shared with Paul Cadbury that the first responsibility of the trustees was to protect the charity's capital, and that had to take precedence over family loyalties to the firm. Paul had to explain this thinking to the chairman of Cadbury, (later Sir) Adrian Cadbury, who was very understanding. Diversification began quietly and slowly. By 2000 the Barrow Cadbury Trust owned no shares in the firm of Cadbury and so later, in 2010, when Cadbury was taken over by the American company Kraft, the value of the Barrow Cadbury Trust's investments was unaffected.

In 2001 Eric Adams retired after 29 years' service. In her tribute to him, Anna Southall gave special praise to his work in Northern Ireland, particularly to the bold move to endow the Fermanagh Trust, his part in setting up the Citizen Organizing Foundation, and his contributions to the Disability programme. He was succeeded by Sukhvinder Kaur Stubbs, who came to the Barrow Cadbury Trust from the Runnymede Trust and was chair of the European Network Against Racism. She immediately used this experience to further the Trust's work in the areas of asylum, immigration and integration. The collective budget in this field stood at £445,000 at the time Sukhvinder was appointed. Among the projects continuing to receive grants from the Trust was Windows for Sudan, which among other work provided support for teenage refugees. Its director, Betty Ogwara, explained that, "For the Sudanese community, newly arrived in the UK, information was the key." Windows for Sudan helped groups of students to set up a network of support, meeting in each other's houses, using their own computers to gather information and sharing it with the Sudanese community across the United Kingdom.

Because so much of the Trust's work involved national and indeed international dimensions, the trustees began to weigh up the arguments and benefits of moving the main office from Birmingham to London. By 2003 they had concluded that a London office would be:

> *… more cost-effective in working with the dispersed groups we support and the national projects, many of which are based in the capital. It will also assist in enabling us to bring this wealth of activity to the attention of the decision-makers.*

What was not going to change were the Trust's core values, which involved, in Anna's words:

> *… being a risk-taker with new initiatives, finding and backing good people, encouraging partnership working and supporting projects in more ways than simply providing grants.*

From 2003 the Trust chose to group its funding into three main programmes: Inclusive Communities; Offending and Early Interventions; and Global Exchange. Each would target projects where the Trust could work in partnership to effect social change.

The move of the office to London was not without misgivings. Trustees believed that much of the strength of the Barrow Cadbury Trust derived from its long association with, and experience of, issues of social justice in the West Midlands and there was a conscious and determined effort among staff and trustees alike to try to ensure that these benefits and strengths were not dissipated. As Sukhvinder recognised, it was that long engagement with the West Midlands that "gives us antennae in the community and enables us to understand what is happening in a way that policy-makers based in London can find difficult."

A constantly recurring theme has been the view of the trustees of their role as supporters and facilitators, working through others. Anthony Wilson had expressed this powerfully in 1993:

> *My respect is for the people on the ground and what they wanted to do. … My respect is certainly for the Trustees, but above all, it's for the people who have been doing the work that it has been our privilege to help. … The whole point of a grant is to liberate people to carry through their concerns, and not to control them. The grant has to be a liberating experience.*

Eric Adams was equally well aware of the importance of having the right structures in place. He once described how a recipient of a grant from the Trust had, at a meeting of his organisation, quoted Seamus Heaney's poem *Scaffolding*, in order to express their appreciation. The words stand as testament to the inspirational lead shown by Barrow and Geraldine Cadbury, by their son Paul and indeed by all those who have dedicated their time and energies to the work of the Barrow Cadbury Trust:

> *Masons, when they start upon a building,*
> *Are careful to test out the scaffolding;*
>
> *Make sure that planks won't slip at busy points,*
> *Secure all ladders, tighten bolted joints.*
>
> *And yet all this comes down when the job's done*
> *Showing off walls of sure and solid stone.*
>
> *So if, my dear, there sometimes seems to be*
> *Old bridges breaking between you and me*
>
> *Never fear. We may let the scaffolds fall*
> *Confident that we have built our wall.*

The first decade of the twenty-first century saw other changes. In 2006 Ruth Cadbury took over as chair, combining the role with her considerable political commitment as initially a councillor, and then deputy leader, of Hounslow Borough Council. Three years later, Sara Llewellin was appointed as chief executive. Throughout, the overriding concern of the Barrow Cadbury Trust has continued to be the pursuit of social justice, the fundamental ideal that underpins four enduring commitments of the Trust: to criminal justice, gender justice, racial justice and economic justice. There is also a growing interest in sustainability issues, which builds on the longstanding Quaker concern with tackling the causes of poverty and not just its symptoms. It was Quakers who, during the Irish Hunger of the 1840s, bought back the nets of Galway fishermen after these had been sold by the men themselves in order to feed their families. It was an act of philanthropy with far more sustainable impact than the simple distribution of food parcels, and for over 150 years has served as an inspiring model for sustainable development. The Trust's interest is still in sustaining resilient communities, and resilient organisations.

Furthering the Trust's programmes involves working with others, as has always been the Trust's policy and practice. In tackling the difficult issues surrounding migration and community cohesion, for example, the Trust seeks to "speak truth to power", both recording the views and experiences of otherwise invisible migrant groups and bringing their stories into the public policy arena. This is achieved by working with the media, through a presence at fringe events during the party conference season, and by building and convening networks of those involved in social justice.

The value of working in a measured and structured way that both harnesses innovation and builds on proven methods of delivering results is central to the Trust's success. Building coalitions and developing infrastructure support for grass-root and campaigning activity are approaches with a long tradition in the Trust's work. Current initiatives seek to build on this inspirational legacy in ways that make a lasting contribution. Acting as a 'midwife' for the Migrants' Rights Network in the 2000s, and – at the time of writing – establishing the new social justice communications organisation British Future to encourage a balanced debate on migration, are just two examples of how the Trust continues to effect change and improve public discourse. The funding collaboration behind this venture has created a new organisation with start-up funds, the intention being to step back at a later point, as is implied in Seamus Heaney's poem.

The Trust is also working on contemporary poverty issues. It was an early sponsor of the 'better banking' campaign, and has used its grants and reputation to campaign for banks to invest in poor communities, as well as for the better regulation of loan-sharking and the need to kickstart local mutual aid projects. Based on the belief that poverty is structural rather than inevitable, the Trust's current programme of anti-poverty work stretches from the global to the local. At the international level it takes the form of funding research into how a more sustainable economic framework can be fostered at a time of global financial crisis. At the local level it includes providing small-scale funding for neighbourhood self-help food co-ops, time banks, sewing clubs and gardening groups, for example.

Work to improve the life chances and rehabilitation of young adult offenders continues in the form of the partnership campaign of the Transition to Adulthood (T2A) Alliance, initiated by the Trust under Anna Southall's chairwomanship. Additionally, work continues with other funders and the Ministry of Justice on how best to assist women on early release from prison and in the community. Much of this activity is a continuation of the ideals of Barrow and Geraldine Cadbury, re-expressed in a contemporary context.

Some areas of work are only possible because of Barrow Cadbury's foresight in establishing the non-charitable Fund. A portion of the endowment is still kept in a tax-paying fund, which can support work that falls outside the legal definition of 'charitable'. The definition of charitable activity broadened considerably with the Charity Act (2006), and the work of both Trust and Fund are non-party political and aim to be even-handed. But where there could be doubt, the Barrow Cadbury Fund can be used to pursue what trustees and directors consider legitimate social justice ends.

Meanwhile, discussion continues on funding strategies and how best to manage the Trust's income versus its capital reserves. The annual report for 2001 noted that a policy had been adopted "to spend each year 5.75 per cent of the Trust's capital value at the end of the previous calendar year." In the current climate, this is clearly unsustainable. The decision to fund grants from capital was debated by the trustees at the time, and consideration given to 'spending out' over a ten- or twenty-year period at one extreme, or of building up their capital reserves at the other. In what Anna Southall recalls as "a rather Quakerly manner," the trustees opted for a middle course. Whether to use capital for grants as well as income,

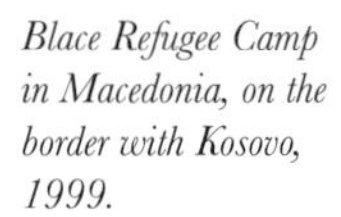

Blace Refugee Camp in Macedonia, on the border with Kosovo, 1999.

T2A: the Transition to Adulthood Alliance, a programme supported by the Barrow Cadbury Trust from 2008 to analyse the problems faced by young adult offenders, and to seek recommendations for change.

rather than maintain its level as endowment, is a recurring issue but one which had not hitherto required addressing directly because of the generous 'topping up' of the endowment by family members through gifts and legacies.

The Barrow Cadbury Trust has been constant in its pursuit of social justice. That search has involved new priorities and reconsidered objectives. It has also demanded a willingness to question and scrutinise the effectiveness of the many grant programmes that have received support. Writing in 2006, in the Barrow Cadbury Trust's ten-year review, *Legacy of Social Justice*, the newly appointed chair, Ruth Cadbury, observed:

> *I think Barrow and Geraldine would be disappointed that there has not been the real shift in 'life chances' that our nation's prosperity since the Second World War should have brought. They would be saddened that the problems they highlighted in the criminal justice system are still prevalent; with the appallingly high rates of mental health problems and substance addiction, and the continuing lack of opportunities for people coming out of prison. Other issues that we now work on, following their founding principles, such as racial justice, migration and asylum, become ever more complex and confused over time.*

But she was able to conclude on an optimistic note, saying how she and her fellow trustees felt privileged to be in a position to carry forward their great-grandparents' work. They are confident that "the Trust will remain true to their vision for generations to come."

Last Word *from The Chair*
Looking Forward

We first conceived of this project as an exercise in documenting the history of the Barrow Cadbury Trust for largely internal purposes. As a family trust, we enable younger family members to take up trusteeship and we recognise the need to capture for them what has hitherto been passed orally from generation to generation. Now we have fifth generation family trustees, not all of whom have been brought up as Quakers or been educated at Quaker schools. They need to understand the values and vision which drove their great-great-grandparents, and work out for themselves what the modern-day manifestation of those values and that vision should be.

Anna Southall is the only current trustee who remembers Barrow, as he lived to a great age. Geraldine, her inspiration, she never met. For four of us – Anna, Ruth, Erica and Helen – Paul was our much-loved Grandpa. We four have served on the trustee board for many years between us and were influenced, either directly or indirectly, by Grandpa Paul's approach. With the next generation of cousins already serving on the Board, and our own children at or approaching the age of potential trusteeship, we wanted them to understand more of the Quaker roots and the social justice values upon which a century of work has been based.

As a governing body, we are the guardians of the Trust's values and vision, a responsibility which we take very seriously. Our job as trustees, after consultation with others, is to set the Trust's strategy for pursuing our vision and mission. We cannot do this without others. Since the 1970s the Trust has employed paid staff and we are very conscious that these are the people who work intensively to achieve our social justice goals. Trustees and staff work together closely to pursue jointly defined goals and our achievements are largely attributable to our staff and funded partners. In 2009 we appointed two non-family trustees to fill particular skills gaps and widen our range of perspectives. This has proved very fruitful and we will continue using this approach. It is important that all trustees and staff understand and share the values of the Trust. Hopefully they will find a written history useful in guiding and inspiring their thinking.

So we embarked on this project to produce a succinct history to illustrate our Quaker roots and our historic attitude to risk and innovation in grant-making and social policy. We wanted future trustees and staff to locate their contribution in an historical and ethical context. What emerged, of course, were fascinating human stories, skilfully teased from interviews and painstakingly uncovered from our extensive archives. We are immensely grateful to Merlin Waterson and Samantha Wyndham for their passion, patience and skill. Their flair and delight in detail, sometimes idiosyncratic, has made this story bubble and fizz with the strength of character of its major protagonists. And yet, even more strikingly than that, the founding values shine through.

Quakers believe that all people are equal in the sight of God, however one conceives God to be. Barrow and Geraldine believed they had a duty to improve the temporal experience of their fellow humans – because they could. They believed deeply in the eighteenth-century Quaker imperative to "speak truth to power" and they modelled for us a fearlessness in doing so. They believed, as do people of faith across the world, in forgiveness and redemption – the basis for their commitment to the rehabilitation of offenders. They also believed in the tradition, so well articulated by family friend and role model Joseph Rowntree, of tackling the root causes of social problems, not just their symptoms.

All these things guide and influence our work to this day. So where are we now and where do we see ourselves going? At the time of writing, we are facing the aftermath of the greatest global financial crash for almost a century. While the purpose of this book is to stand back from the particularity of the moment and take a broader look at how values both endure and adapt through time, nevertheless we want to bring the narrative of our work up to date.

Our current chief executive, Sara Llewellin, brought to the Trust her long history of social justice activism and a specific interest in social investment. This has helped the Trust build on earlier work, including that by Sukhvinder Kaur Stubbs, which had resulted in the establishment of the Commission on Young Adults in the Criminal Justice System (2003–05) and its report, *Lost In Transition.* This led directly to the establishment of the Transition to Adulthood Alliance (T2A), a broad coalition of organisations working to identify and promote the adoption of a distinct approach to young adults in the criminal justice system, one that is proportionate to their maturity and responsive to their specific needs. The Alliance is now achieving impact both at the national policy level and in local service commissioning and delivery.

T2A marks the deepening understanding of partnership working and its potential for social justice change. Although we have always worked with others, listening carefully to the views and analysis of funded partners, T2A still broke new ground for us. By brokering an alliance of powerful voices and differing perspectives on young adults and the penal system, from practitioners, policy analysts and campaigners, we created something bigger than ourselves and which took on an identity of its own, assisted – but not driven – by our funding. Now the Alliance sets its own annual strategy, which we as a board of trustees endorse, and the programme funding is used to deliver a strategy that is agreed collectively and is not simply of our own making.

As already explained, the move to London was not made without considerable heart-searching. Barrow, Geraldine and Paul were all key figures in Birmingham civic life and felt passionately about the city and its people. Times change, however, and in the modern day it is undoubtedly easier to influence public policy from a London base. Indeed, our relative success to date in getting closer to policy-makers and achieving greater impact on policy and public discourse convinces us that we did the right thing.

Importantly, we still work closely with Birmingham's voluntary and community sectors and maintain links with the city's major civic organisations. We remain active members of Charitable Trusts West Midlands and support the work of the Lunar Society in bringing innovators, thinkers and leaders together. Our model is to commission and fund public policy research in our programme areas and to feed into that work the experiences and voices of people working 'on the ground'. Sometimes this takes the form of action research involving grass-roots community organisations. With the majority of our partner researchers and think-tanks based in London, and the majority of our grass-roots funding going to groups in Birmingham and the Black Country, this model of working can bring the voices of Birmingham people into the national policy arena. Current examples of this linkage are research projects on community resilience by Demos, the Young Foundation and new economics foundation (nef). All have, or will have, findings of national significance and all focus on neighbourhoods in Birmingham. We consider this a creative and intelligent way to pursue our concerns for fairer public policy while honouring our Birmingham roots and benefiting the people of that city.

Partnerships and collaborations take time, effort and resources. While not suitable for every kind of project, they are often our preferred way of working. We are very aware of the need for independent funders like ourselves to consider our mandate, and we consult widely with practitioners and campaigners about what socially just change should or could look like. We know the Trust's endowment, while certainly a treasured part of our family heritage, is not 'our' money, but a resource held in trust by us for the common good, for the pursuit of equality and justice. We cannot achieve much on our own and we would be foolish to try. Apart from anything else, we simply do not have enough money. But funding aside, we want to broker and bring about change by standing alongside the real experts: community activists, leaders and campaigners who have vision, courage and verve. We want not only to put money into their hands, but to strengthen those hands.

As has been amply illustrated in this account of our history, the Trust has a long tradition of what are now termed 'funder-plus' approaches. For us, this is about both strengthening civil society – by helping organisations do what they do better – and building alliances for socially just change. Sometimes it requires us to follow the experts and make sure they have the resources they need at critical times. An example was the core funding we gave to the Fawcett Society to assist their Judicial Review (2010) into the government's failure to take full account of the disproportionate impact their economic austerity plans would have on women. At other times it requires us to join forces with other funders to magnify our voices for change, an example being the Corston Independent Funders' Coalition – over 20 foundations hiring an advocate and driving a campaign for the implementation of Baroness Corston's recommendations regarding the treatment of women in the criminal justice system.

The amount of money available to us is not huge. Our endowment stands at between £70–80 million and our current annual spend at £4 million. At the present time we are spending more than our income, a deliberate and strategic choice on our part. First, we take the view that it is important to maintain our programmes and grant-making in times of economic downturn through what is known as 'counter-cyclical giving'. Second, and equally important, our criminal justice work and T2A in particular have now built up to the point where we are making real progress in influencing policy and in the vital dissemination of our findings from demonstration models. Now would be a foolish and wasteful time to cut back on that work.

Our current programmes are the modern-day iteration of the Trust's commitment to social justice:

> *Criminal Justice*: focusing on young adults in the penal system, the particular needs of women, and diverting young people from gangs and crime.

Migration and Europe: focusing on achieving a migration policy which is fair to migrants and to host communities, on promoting good practice in integration, and on encouraging a healthier public discourse about migration.

Poverty and Inclusion: focusing on sustainable and fair economic policy, financial inclusion and community resilience.

In all our programmes we attempt to identify the most pressing issues and work with others to achieve beneficial change. We support and work with think-tanks across the political spectrum, believing that no single perspective, manifesto or creed has a monopoly of good ideas, solutions or moral authority. We do, however, unashamedly seek and advocate a more equal and fairer society based on the intrinsic dignity and value of all people.

Our aim as a social justice foundation is to catalyse socially just change with every injection of funding we make, whether that be large or small, grant or investment, acting together with others or working alone. We no longer think so much of 'fewer and larger' but rather 'what change in the world will this catalyse or achieve?'.

As a trust with Quaker origins, we have always had an ethical approach to the management of our endowment. We have observed the usual negative screening to avoid investing in harm, such as companies trading in tobacco, armaments or colluding with human rights abuses. Now we are going further and developing a more proactive approach to using up to five per cent of our capital for mission-related impact. Along with a number of other foundations in the UK, we have started to use some of our endowment for social impact investing. We believe that by investing in projects that offer a social as well as a financial return we can 'recycle' our money and pursue our mission at the same time. More importantly, as a small player, we want to help catalyse this marketplace for mainstream investors.

As we conclude what has been a fascinating journey from the inception of this project to the publication of this book, we reflect on the strength of character, creativity and resilience of so many of the Trust's funded partners through the decades. We are the broker of change, the middle man. We put resources into the hands of changemakers and if they make the world a better place, the credit is all theirs. We are proud to support them and we thank them greatly.

What about the longer-term future of the Barrow Cadbury Trust? We will consider periodically the issue of perpetuity versus spend down, but more importantly, we will continue to update and refresh our understanding of what socially just change looks like and renew our strategy for achieving it. Like any other charity, we have a duty to pursue our mission vigorously. For us, giving money away is a means, not an end. We exist not to dispense largesse but to use all the resources at our disposal carefully and thoughtfully to bring about beneficial change. To get behind inspirational people and ideas and boldly to take risks.

Some of the stories told in this book have made us ask the questions afresh: "Are we being bold enough?", "Are we fleet of foot?" and, most importantly of all, "Are we creating opportunities for marginalised people to speak truth to power?" These are questions with which we will regularly challenge ourselves. What we do know is that any major decisions the board makes, now or in the future, will be in pursuit of our vision of "a peaceful, equitable society, free from discrimination and based on the principle of social justice for all", and in honour of our founders, Barrow and Geraldine.

Ruth Cadbury and Anna Southall
Winter 2012

Left *Anna C Southall, trustee of the Barrow & Geraldine S Cadbury Trust since 1973, and chairwoman of the Barrow Cadbury Trust from 1996 to 2006;* Right *Ruth M Cadbury, trustee of the Barrow & Geraldine S Cadbury Trust from 1980 and chair of the Barrow Cadbury Trust since 2006. Both are great-granddaughters of Barrow and Geraldine Cadbury.*

Trustee Tree

Entries shown in grey appear in the book but were not trustees.

JOHN CADBURY = (m., as 2nd wife, in 1832) CANDIA (BARROW) CADBURY
1801–89
Tea and chocolate manufacturer of Birmingham
Founder of Cadbury Bros

1805–55

RICHARD CADBURY = (m., as 1st wife, in 1861) ELIZABETH (ADLINGTON) CADBURY
1835–99
Partner in Cadbury Bros

1838–68

BARROW CADBURY = (m. in 1891) GERALDINE (SOUTHALL) CADBURY
1862–1958
Chairman of British Cocoa and Chocolate Co. Founder of the Barrow & Geraldine S Cadbury Trust in 1920 and the Barrow Cadbury Fund Ltd in 1924 (and chairman of both from their foundation until his death)

1865–1941
Trustee of both the Barrow & Geraldine S Cadbury Trust and of the Barrow Cadbury Fund from their foundation to her death

DOROTHY ADLINGTON CADBURY
1892–1987
Trustee of the Barrow & Geraldine S Cadbury Trust from 1934 to 1987

PAUL STRANGMAN CADBURY = (m. in 1919) RACHEL EVELINE (WILSON) CADBURY
1895–1984
Chairman of Cadbury Bros and chairman of the Friends' Ambulance Unit Council. Trustee of the Barrow & Geraldine S Cadbury Trust from 1934 to 1984 (and chairman from 1958 to 1984); founder of the Paul S Cadbury Charitable Trust in 1931 (and chairman from then until his death)

1894–1993
Trustee of the Barrow & Geraldine S Cadbury Trust from 1944 to 1993

CATHERINE RACHEL (CADBURY) HICKINBOTHAM
b.1920
Trustee of the Barrow & Geraldine S Cadbury Trust from 1959 to 1996, and chairman of it (as well as of the Barrow Cadbury Fund and the Paul S Cadbury Trust) from 1984 to 1993

EDWARD PAUL CADBURY
1921–2002
Trustee of the Barrow & Geraldine S Cadbury Trust from 1959 to 1996

ROGER PAUL HICKINBOTHAM
b.1948
Trustee of the Barrow Cadbury Trust from 1978 to 2008

RICHARD GEOFFREY CADBURY
b.1949
Trustee of the Barrow Cadbury Trust from 1978 to 2003

JAMES EDWARD CADBURY
b.1951
Trustee of the Barrow Cadbury Trust from 1985 to 2008 and deputy chairman from 1997 to 2006

ERICA RACHEL CADBURY
b.1957
Trustee of the Barrow Cadbury Trust since 1983

ANNA (HICKINBOTHAM) STEIGER
b.1978
Trustee of the Barrow Cadbury Trust from 2002 to 2011

TAMSIN RUPPRECHTER
b.1976 (granddaughter of Catherine Hickinbotham)
Trustee of the Barrow Cadbury Trust since 2007

NICOLA CADBURY
b.1975
Trustee of the Barrow Cadbury Trust since 1998

Other trustees:

RICHARD BRENNAN
1952–2010
Trustee of the Barrow Cadbury Trust from 2009 to 2010

GORDON MITCHELL
b.1956
Trustee of the Barrow Cadbury Trust since 2009

Notes:

1. All family trustees of the Barrow & Geraldine S Cadbury Trust and Barrow Cadbury Trust were also appointed as directors of the Barrow Cadbury Fund until its incorporation in June 2006.

2. All trustee descendants of Paul and Rachel Cadbury were also trustees of the Paul S Cadbury Trust until the amalgamation of the trusts to form the Barrow Cadbury Trust in 1994.

GERALDINE ('CHERRY') MARY CADBURY
1900–99
Trustee of the Barrow & Geraldine S Cadbury Trust from 1934 to 1994

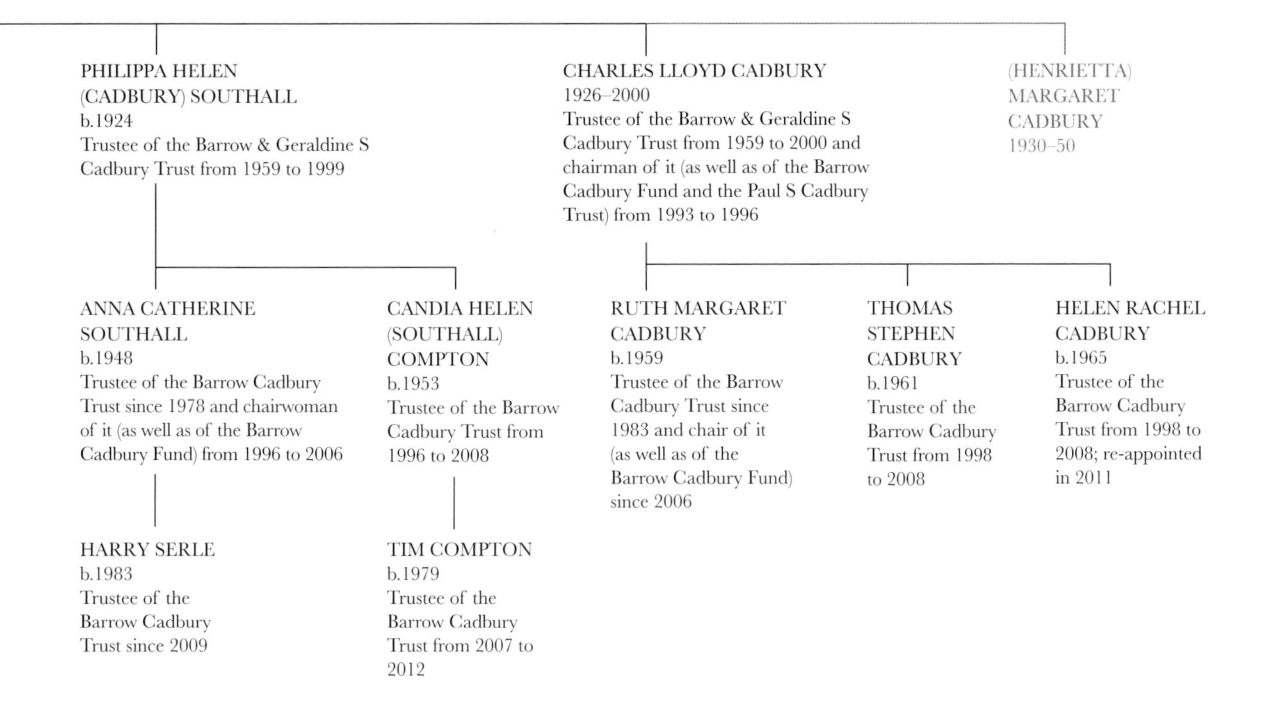

The family party held to celebrate Barrow Cadbury's 95th birthday in 1957.

Back row, left to right: *Catherine Hickinbotham, Charles Cadbury, Jillian Ransome (later Cadbury), Edward Cadbury, Philippa Southall, Stephen Southall, Paul Hickinbotham;*

Middle row, left to right: *Anna Southall, Paul Cadbury, Mary Cadbury (with Erica Cadbury on her knee), Rachel Cadbury, Barrow Cadbury, Helen Dixon (one of Barrow's half-sisters), Dorothy Cadbury, Geraldine Cadbury, Claire Hickinbotham;* Front row, left to right: *Candia Southall, Richard Cadbury, James Cadbury, Roger Hickinbotham, Mark Southall, Philip Cadbury*

Sources and select bibliography

Archives

The archives of the Barrow & Geraldine S Cadbury Trust, the Paul S Cadbury Trust and the Barrow Cadbury Fund Ltd are held by the Archives & Heritage Department of Birmingham Central Library, under the accession number MS 1579. They date from the original deeds establishing the Barrow & Geraldine S Cadbury Trust and the Barrow Cadbury Fund Ltd in the early 1920s through to about 2005, and include annual reports, minute books and numerous grant files, although many of the latter are either accessible only with the prior permission of the trustees of the Barrow Cadbury Trust or are currently closed under data protection legislation. The library holds a brief list of the accession dates and deposits made to the archives by the Barrow Cadbury Trust since 1989, but there is currently no full catalogue of this collection.

At the time of going to press the Trust has just appointed an archivist, who will spend eighteen months cataloguing the archive collection under the expert guidance of the Archives & Heritage Department of Birmingham Central Library. It is anticipated that the collection will be accessible and navigable from 2014.

The Library of the Religious Society of Friends, located at Friends' House, 173–177 Euston Road, London NW1, is one of the largest collections in the world of printed material relating to Quakers. Founded in 1673, it is an invaluable resource for information on individuals, as well as on Quaker history, faith, thought and practice in the fields of peace, prison reform, humanitarian assistance and the anti-slavery movement.

Paul Cadbury's unpublished *An Account of Three Charitable Trusts and a Benevolent Company* (1971) is particularly valuable. Copies are held by the Barrow Cadbury Trust and Birmingham Central Library (ref. MS 1579).

Interviews

Transcriptions of the following interviews, conducted for this publication, have been deposited with the Barrow Cadbury Trust:

Eric Adams, 7 September 2010
Sir Adrian Cadbury, 6 July 2010
Catherine Rachel Hickinbotham (*née* Cadbury)
and Philippa Helen Southall (*née* Cadbury), 25 February 2010
Sara Llewellin, 7 December 2010
Anna Southall, 20 July 2010 and 23 February 2011
Anthony Wilson, 6 September 2010
Dipali Chandra, 6 March 2012

Published Articles and Books

Bartlett, Percy W, *Barrow Cadbury: a memoir* (London, 1960).
Briggs, Asa, *Social Thought and Social Action: a study of the work of Seebohm Rowntree* (London, 1961).
Cadbury, Deborah, *Chocolate Wars: From Cadbury to Kraft – 200 years of Sweet Success and Bitter Rivalry* (London, 2010).
Cadbury, Geraldine, *Young Offenders Yesterday and Today* (London, 1938).
Chinn, Carl, *The Cadbury Story* (Studley, 1998).
Davies, A Tegla, *Friends' Ambulance Unit: the story of the FAU in the Second World War 1939–1946* (London, 1947).
Freeman, Mark, *The Joseph Rowntree Charitable Trust: A Study in Quaker Philanthropy and Adult Education 1904–1954* (York, 2004).
Fry, A Ruth, *Quaker Ways* (Watford, 1933).
Kennedy, Thomas C, *British Quakerism 1860–1920: The Transformation of a Religious Community* (Oxford, 2001).
Lloyd, Humphrey, *The Quaker Lloyds in the Industrial Revolution* (London, 1975).
Owen, David, *English Philanthropy 1660–1960* (Oxford, 1965).
Raistrick, Arthur, *Quakers in Science and Industry* (Newton Abbot, 1968).
Waddilove, Lewis E, *Private Philanthropy and Public Welfare: the Joseph Rowntree Memorial Trust 1954–1973* (London, 1983).
Whitney, Janet, *Geraldine S Cadbury 1865–1941: A Biography* (London, 1948).
Wilmot, Frances & Saul, Pauline, *A Breath of Fresh Air: Birmingham's Open-Air Schools 1911–1970* (Chichester, 1998).

Index

Page numbers in *italics* refer to illustrations

Acknowledgements and picture credits

In the summer of 2009 the Trustees of the Barrow Cadbury Trust decided to commission a short history. Their intention was to provide an account of how the Trust had developed since it was formed by Barrow Cadbury in 1920. The principal aim was to help Trustees and staff decide where the Trust should be going, on the basis of a fuller understanding of where it had come from. It was also hoped that the history would be useful to all those with an interest in the changing face of Quaker philanthropy.

The decision to entrust the history to us was made in January 2010. In the course of the following year a mass of archival and other material was made available. Our first debt of gratitude is to the Trustees for not only asking us to undertake the task, but for their interest and encouragement at every stage of the project. We are particularly grateful for all the time given by Anna Southall, and for her many stimulating insights, recorded in two long interviews.

We have also been supported and helped by the staff of the Trust. Susie Parsons, the acting Chief Executive, initially approached us with an admirably succinct brief. From the moment that Sara Llewellin took up the reins she has been exceptionally generous with her time and guidance. The help we have received from Sharon Wellington and Madeleine Rooke-Ley is also greatly appreciated.

Part of our brief was to record those who had helped to shape the Trust during the second half of the twentieth century. We were welcomed with extraordinary kindness by Catherine Hickinbotham, Philippa Southall, Sir Adrian Cadbury, Anthony Wilson and Eric Adams, and greatly enjoyed meeting Dipali Chandra.

The archives of the Trust have largely been transferred to Birmingham Central Library. We are grateful to the staff there, and to those who assisted us in the library of Friends' House (built with generous support from Barrow Cadbury), and at the London Library.

Our special thanks go to James Parry for steering the book so skilfully through its various stages, and to Matt Bourne for his elegant but Quakerish design.

This project has proved to be an enjoyable, enriching and fascinating one. Something of that is, we hope, conveyed in our account of the history of the Trust.

Merlin Waterson and Samantha Wyndham
Winter 2012

Picture credits

Asian Resource Centre, Birmingham/Aftab Rahman, p.94; Bank of England, p.16; Barrow Cadbury Trust, pp.102, 123, 129; Birmingham Disability Resource Centre, pp.77, 79; Birmingham Education Department, p.34; Reproduced with the permission of Birmingham Libraries & Archives, pp.28, 31 (photograph by Gudrun Limbrick), 40, 52, 53 (photograph by Tom McCormick); ©Birmingham Museums and Art Gallery, p.113; Bournville Village Trust, p.25; Colin Baker (photograph by Arthur Wells), p.29; Corrymeela Community, Co. Antrim, pp.89, 90 (photograph by The Fashion Souk, Belfast); Fermanagh Trust, Enniskillen, Co. Fermanagh, p.105; Getty Images, p.23; ©Howard Davies (reportdigital.co.uk), p.122; ©Hulton-Deutsch Collection/CORBIS, p.108; Hunter's Hill School, Birmingham, p.41 (top and bottom); Ironbridge Gorge Museum Trust, p.75; Kraft Foods UK, (http://www.cadburyworld.co.uk), pp.2, 8, 10, 12; ©Mount Pleasant School Farm, Birmingham, p.71; ©National Portrait Gallery, London, p.45; ©National Trust Images/David Noton, Image ref. 47672, pp.56–57; Oosoom (2007) http://en.wikipedia.org, p.24; Private Collection/Barrow Cadbury Trust, pp.4, 6, 7, 11, 13, 14, 15, 18, 19, 26, 27, 32, 43 (photograph by Ernest H Fletcher, Moseley), 50, 54, 55, 65, 70, 73 (left and right), 84, 97, 104, 132–133; ©Religious Society of Friends in Britain, pp.46–47, 59, 60, 61 (top and bottom), 62, 63, 64, 66, 68; Ruskin Museum, Coniston, Cumbria, UK/Bridgeman Art Library, London, p.21; Sampad South Asian Arts, Birmingham (photograph by Eric Richmond), p.115; Uffculme School, Birmingham, p.35; Westhill Endowment Trust, Birmingham, p.39; http://commons.wikimedia.org/wiki/File:George_Bell_1931.jpg, p.109; ©with and beans/Alamy, p.92; Woodbrooke Quaker Study Centre, Birmingham, p.36. On p.120, the section of Seamus Heaney's poem *Scaffolding* is reproduced by kind permission of Faber and Faber Ltd.

First published in 2013 by The Barrow Cadbury Trust
Kean House, 6 Kean Street, London WC2B 4AS
Registered Charity Number: 1115476

www.barrowcadbury.org.uk

ISBN 978-0-9574840-0-9

Editor James Parry www.jamesvparry.com
Design and layout LEVEL www.levelpartnership.co.uk
Printed and bound by Empress Litho